FATHER'S DAY

FATHER'S DAY

Steven Schnur

Illustrated by Cheryl Gross

(Previously published in hardcover as *DADDY'S HOME!*)

AVON BOOKS ◆ NEW YORK

This book was originally published in hardcover as *Daddy's Home!*

Portions of this book were previously published in *The New York Times*. Copyright © 1984, 1985, 1986, 1987, 1988, 1989 by The New York Times Company. Reprinted by permission of *The New York Times*.

AVON BOOKS
A division of
The Hearst Corporation
105 Madison Avenue
New York, New York 10016

Copyright © 1990 by Steven Schnur
Cover art by Chris Spollen
Published by arrangement with Crown Publishers, Inc.
Library of Congress Catalog Card Number: 89-25273
ISBN: 0-380-71454-X

The Crown Publishers, Inc. edition contains the following Library of Congress Cataloging in Publication Data:

Schnur, Steven.
    Daddy's home! : reflections of a family man / Steven Schnur.—1st ed.
    p.   cm.
1. Schnur, Steven.   2. Fathers—United States—Biography.
3. Parenthood—United States.   I. Title.
HQ756.S36   1990
306.874′2′092—dc20   89-25273
                                                                                              CIP

First Avon Books Trade Printing: June 1991

AVON TRADEMARK REG. U.S. PAT. OFF. AND IN OTHER COUNTRIES, MARCA REGISTRADA, HECHO EN U.S.A.

Printed in the U.S.A.

OPM 10 9 8 7 6 5 4 3 2 1

For Nancie
with eternal gratitude
and abiding love

FATHER'S DAY

CONTENTS

FATHER'S
DAY

INTRODUCTION

Thirty years ago, in a quiet suburb on Long Island Sound, I borrowed a rowboat from a neighbor's beach, dragged it with the help of a friend over rocky shoals at low tide, and slid noiselessly into the shallow waters of a nearby cove. It was the first significant mischief in my seven years of life. I had every intention of returning the boat before its owner came home from work. My friend and I did not wish to be caught in our trespass, we simply sought to transform the lethargy of a blistering August afternoon into adventure on the high seas.

But because neither of us knew how to use the oarlocks, sitting one behind the other as if in a canoe, we never reached the low stone bridge separating our inlet from open water. Instead we paddled erratically from shore to shore, twice running aground before being driven back by strong currents as the tide reversed and the dark green waters of the sound began flooding back into our cove. Though we escaped detection and discipline that afternoon, I never forgot our episode of petty larceny, not for the fear of punishment it induced, but as a result of discovering that my friend was fatherless.

I was startled by the admission, too absorbed in the freedoms of that first summer of boyhood independence to notice his father's absence. In all the months we had played together he had never so much as hinted at the loss. Perhaps the subject caused him great pain; more likely, he understood instinctively that I would pity him. I did. From that moment I thought of him as in some way crippled, limbless, lacking what the rest of us had, what we took for granted. Yet he neither openly mourned nor actively lamented his fate. Indeed, what impressed me most that afternoon as we paddled in circles under the scorching sun was his seeming indifference to this misfortune.

He had few memories of his father, no heroic stories, no tales of fishing or ball playing. What he remembered most were the barbecues. "Sometimes he'd stand out under an umbrella, grilling in the rain," he told me flatly. Three years after his father's death nothing aroused images of him with greater immediacy than the smell of charcoal.

When I asked how his father had died, Michael shrugged, repeating what he had heard whispered about for three years: cancer. My parents, in the hushed voice reserved for family secrets and terminal illness, later revealed that Michael's father had died of leukemia at the age of thirty-two. His relative youth meant nothing to me then; I lumped all fathers together, regardless of age. But though unable to feel for him, I was chilled by the abandonment of his son. What was it like to be fatherless? I wondered, trying occasionally to draw my friend out. "It's alright, I guess," he would answer, either unwilling to reveal his inmost emotions or not yet ready to probe them. Fatherlessness was what he knew, what he had known for almost half his life; he took it for granted.

I never asked him if he had loved his father; I assumed he must have, especially in his absence. But after trying to draw out his memories I realized he could hardly love what he had barely known, unable to recall either the color of his father's eyes or the sound of his voice. With the exception of a few photographs on the piano and half a dozen letters to his wife, the man had left nothing of himself behind.

I never thought to pity Michael's father, robbed of life just when it had the most to offer. To be a father was, by definition, to be old, to have lived a long life. Eventually all fathers died. It was the price they paid for age and for children. What troubled me was not the injustice of his passing, but the absence of a protector and provider for my friend. Michael seemed exposed and vulnerable in ways the rest of us were not. His mother—no mother—could fill such a void.

The following summer my family moved from that waterfront community. Sometime later his mother remarried and took him away as well. Out of touch and gradually displaced in my affections by new friends, he disappeared from my thoughts for nearly two decades until marriage and the birth of my own children thrust him back into consciousness. Then my sympathies began to hover not over him but his unfortunate father. A siren of interrupted parenthood, the faceless man hailed me one quiet evening from a vague and distant shore, whispering his regrets, his deep sadness at leaving nothing behind that might have spoken to his son, no ethical will, no diary, no simple statement of his hopes and fears. Michael, he lamented in our moment of communion, could only guess at the man who had fathered him.

That night I determined to leave behind something more of myself than merely the image of umbrellas and the aroma of charcoal, something of my thoughts, a sense of the past. I would not try to tell my life story, I decided, but rather concentrate on those kernels of intense feeling that so animated my life—the moments of sudden incandescence that fatherhood was making almost commonplace. On such occasions I seemed to inflate beyond the normal boundaries of the self, to find in the natural world confirmation of my own infatuation with life and reverence for death. I had no vision then of the unity of such moments, just an overwhelming thankfulness for the birth of my children and the desire to preserve that gratitude. In crystallizing those prayerful moments, I hoped to leave behind a meaningful trace of myself, a map of my mind.

Repeatedly during recent years, the image of the rowboat has returned to me, only now it holds not my childhood friend but my burgeoning family, the five of us paddling not against the emerald waters of the sound, but against the rising tide of time. Sooner or later, I know, we will have to put into shore, the summer will end, we will all disperse. With that day in mind I have attempted to preserve in words what is so fleeting in nature: the cherished hopes, the mayhem, and the minor miracles that amplify the narrowly circumscribed universe of one doting father.

FIRST FRUITS

INFERTILITY

My wife, her legs wrapped in an afghan, is sitting beside the fire knitting, and I have just put down my book to watch her. She never knit before and until a few weeks ago never so much as expressed an interest in learning. But three months from now our first child is due, and suddenly much has begun to change in our lives, particularly the frequency with which tears well up in my eyes.

We always thought of ourselves as a modern couple, marrying in our mid-twenties, deferring children until our thirties, working long days in Manhattan, eating out most nights. Neither of us knew the difference between baking and broiling, darning and basting; we paid someone to clean up after us; and on rare visits to the supermarket came home with nothing more than orange juice and ice cream.

But as our friends began having children we discovered new pleasures in visiting them. The muted chaos of family life was beginning to exercise its own vague appeal upon us. Still, we were glad to return home to the quiet of each other. Our careers were only just beginning to blossom, hardly the time to give up all we had worked for. We would have kids someday, but not yet, not in the face of so many impending opportunities. And what was the rush? Wasn't it better to have children later in life, when we could provide a more stable environment and look back without regret, careers established, traveling done, our future secure?

And then suddenly, hormonally, children became a need, a hunger. I felt them in the tips of my fingers, dreamed of them nightly. We began to create the idea of parenthood for ourselves, discovering a whole universe of unexplored feelings and paraphernalia. Over pizza we discussed how we would "swing it," how two professional people would raise a child. There were so many obstacles to overcome, so much that had to be sacrificed. Then one night we clung to each other with especial warmth and decided the time had come.

But it hadn't, not that month and not the next. Six months later we made our first medical inquiries and were advised to wait a year before beginning a thorough workup. We waited without result and finally began two years of discomforting fertility tests, holding our breath as each cycle ended, praying for success, then tallying up the accrued bitterness and railing at fate. What had been so insignificant in our lives a year ago was now essential for our happiness. Without children we could no longer feel fulfilled. Our careers began to seem hollow; the pleasure we had taken in our friends' children turned to pain.

We passed through periods of resignation, hope, and combative indifference, determined to get on with life and not succumb to self-pity. But each time failure announced itself Nancie would grow teary and I would sulk off to another room contemplating adoption. How could we who seemed so healthy be the victims of such dysfunction? Infertility was for old childless couples, not young ones like us. After a day or two the disappointment would ebb and we would decide anew that the problem was one of timing. We

20

had simply missed a crucial day during the cycle. The refrain was always the same: "This month for sure."

Pregnancy finally did come, but then so did miscarriage three months later, leaving us back where we started. New tests followed another year of infertility and our conversation turned less to child rearing and increasingly to artificial insemination, in vitro fertilization, adoption, and the astonishing number of couples our age unable to conceive. Perhaps this was the price we had to pay for consuming so much fast food and irradiated milk as

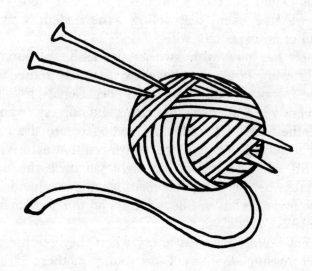

children. We grew to feel abnormal, isolated. How come so many ignorant sixteen-year-olds could conceive and we couldn't? Where was the justice in our being denied our fondest dream while lunatic mothers drowned their babies? Finally, after a particularly painful series of examinations, Nancie declared she was finished with the tests and would accept her fate. We will have a child, she insisted, there is nothing wrong with us.

And then miraculously she was pregnant again and overnight our world changed. At first we tried to protect ourselves from disappointment, remembering the last pregnancy and the years of failure, but as weeks turned to months and months into trimesters we passed from fear to security, realizing we were well on our way to parenthood. Changes began to come so swiftly that I lost sight of the couple we had been, discovering a new identity as the husband of an expectant wife.

I watch her now with awe as she ambles around the house growing larger by the week. She has retired from full-time work, taking only an occasional free-lance assignment when she isn't decorating the nursery or buying baby clothes. Often I find her standing before the mirror smiling at her marvelous shape, convinced that nature has a wonderful sense of humor. At night we track the baby's kicks across her swelling abdomen, placing our hands over the tiny, invisible limbs. She will miss all this movement in three months, she says.

It is not seemly for men to cry when they see pregnant women crossing the street or young mothers strolling infants through the park, but I have grown so sentimental of late that tears come to my eyes more frequently than I can count. Strangers smile at me as I walk to the train. I guess my joy is showing. When friends ask how I am, I have to restrain my delight. How am I? I'm flying! Every night at dinner we bubble over our future, counting the days until our child is due.

The pain is forgotten now, supplanted by a new vitality in the midst of a special fragility. We have shortened our Sunday walks and when Nancie climbs steps I am usually behind her, a supporting hand on her lower back. It is as though she has suddenly aged, a premonition of our future life together. But only her body has slowed; her face reflects the special light of expectancy, an ageless light of great beauty and serenity.

I see that light now, watching her knit a blanket for the crib, looking like every mother who ever feathered the nest of her firstborn. And suddenly the tears are running from my eyes again and she looks up and smiles.

ENDLESS EXPECTANCY

Two weeks ago our obstetrician assured us it could happen any time now. And each night for those two weeks we have gone to sleep wondering if we just spent the last childless day of our lives. But the days pass, Nancie grows larger, and still we wait, poised upon a great bubble of expectancy, attuned as never before to her every abdominal twinge, to every celestial sign, even to our every fortune cookie, searching for the beginning of the thread that will lead us to that mystical realm where babies are born.

We know that due dates are a fiction of anxious parents and accommodating doctors, that infants care little for such calculations, firstborn children especially. Still, for nine months we focused our energies on that day as the most likely arrival time, never considering the consequences of our assumption. Then last Friday it passed and we found ourselves entering a mapless domain of terrifying uncertainty—the tenth month of pregnancy.

Each morning I ride the train to work unable to concentrate on the newspaper, wondering if Nancie has gone into labor during my absence. To be out of reach of a telephone, even for only an hour, is agony. Although a certain measure of calm returns when I reach my office, it vanishes as soon as the phone rings. Has the moment finally arrived? Will I make it home in time? I know that first children are supposed to be slow in coming. But Teflon births seem to run in our family.

Since last Friday I have had to stop making all phone calls. For weeks I aroused explosive expectations in every friend or relative I spoke to. As we approached our due date the hysteria in their voices became so pronounced that I felt guilty causing so much baseless excitement. Then I discovered my movements were being monitored. When I arrived at work half an hour late one morning, my colleagues accused me of deliberately deceiving them, of toying with their emotions. They were certain I had taken Nancie to the hospital. What else would account for my absence? A late train, I said sheepishly. Poor excuse, they answered with annoyance.

To relieve my anxiety I speak with Nancie half a dozen times a day, reviewing our strategies for getting to the hospital, what we should pack in our Lamaze bag, and whom we will call once the baby is born. Over the phone and over dinner we talk about names, still undecided after

nine months. Every week a new favorite supplants the previous one or a relative gives birth and steals our latest choice. I now understand those parents who spend their three days in the hospital avoiding the clerk in charge of registering births. A rose by any other name is simply not a rose. We want to get it right.

Wasn't it only yesterday I left the obstetrician's office yelling to strangers, "We're pregnant!" How distant birth seemed then. As the initial euphoria wore off we realized what a blessing those nine months were. It would take at least that long to acclimate ourselves to the notion of parenthood, to wallpaper the nursery, assemble the crib, and stock up on disposable diapers. But as we approached our due date, the house still in disarray, we began to feel that even nine months was not sufficient time. Elephants had a more reasonable gestation period. Two years would just about do. Then, miraculously, with three weeks to spare, the baby's room was completed, the closets cleaned, even a leaky faucet repaired, and we sat in the midst of rattles, music boxes, and teddy bears congratulating ourselves and the lucky child about to take possession of it all.

On the eve of our due date we drove to the local Chinese restaurant, hoping to prove the old wives' tale that egg rolls, wonton soup, and spare ribs induce labor. It was not the first time we had tried to give our child a little push. In fact, we already had accumulated a dashboard full of fortunes including one that promised, BIG NEWS AWAITS YOU. An hour later we waddled out of the restaurant, both feeling as though we were about to go into labor. Neither of us did. Instead, Nancie awoke at three in the morning with hunger pangs as severe as those she had suffered during her first months of pregnancy. When you enter your tenth month, she told me between spoonfuls of chopped herring, you start pregnancy all over again.

After the Chinese food failed, we turned to spaghetti and meatballs, another favorite of old wives—and equally effective. Then we tried dancing, driving over rutted roads, and whispering magical incantations over Nancie's belly. Finally, we looked up the next full moon, a day most maternity wards are overcrowded. Discovering it was not to occur for two weeks, we both groaned. In our present condition, twenty-four hours is an eternity.

Four days have passed since our due date and still we drift along without bearings, beyond expectancy, on hold. Some nights I hear phantom crying from the nursery; Nancie dreams regularly of clocks sliding down chutes. Where does the mysterious force reside that will one day proclaim an end to our waiting, finally allowing us to become parents? Nothing we do seems to influence it. All it takes is a rush of water and an infant's cry, but still we wait, the day so long anticipated now discarded, some unknown date moving into position to become our child's birthday.

There are moments in the course of this prenatal twilight when I cease thinking about parenthood. Perhaps it will never come, or perhaps it came and we somehow missed it. With each additional day it becomes easier to believe that life will continue just as it has, the two of us waiting, perpetually waiting for children. Nancie had another checkup yesterday and again the doctor told her, "Any time now," assuring her that the one certainty about pregnancy is that it can't last forever. I used to believe that, but lately have begun to wonder.

My Sister, My Daughter

I had just turned sixteen when my parents took me aside one evening, turned down the volume on the television, and explained that I had once had a sister. I stared at the silent screen wondering how I should feel, as unsettled by the revelation as if I had just been told I was adopted. In that moment history seemed to undergo a vast and permanent alteration, though nothing had changed but my perception of it. I was to spend the next sixteen years in search of my sister, trying to recover a past that had been played out long before my birth.

She had been their first child, born into shattering stillness, without sound, without movement, without life. So that was what was meant by stillbirth, I realized, picturing the motionless infant, my nameless sister, lying in the doctor's unwilling hands, born into death. And that was why from time to time my mother had talked about her "first pregnancy," a phrase that had always struck me as odd since she usually referred to her pregnancies by the names of her four sons. Suddenly her often-expressed wish for a daughter took on a new poignancy. I threw my arms around her and said I hoped we four boys had not disappointed her. Through red eyes she smiled and said she was grateful for the longing that had impelled her to try again and again to re-create her lost daughter.

I never talked of my sister, not with my brothers, not even with my parents. But from the moment I learned of her she entered my heart, and there I wove a little life for her. She would have been four years older than I, born into another decade, a child of the late 1940s, blue eyed and fair like my mother. Friends of mine had older sisters, usually aloof, often annoyed by the antics of their little brothers. Would she have felt that way about me? I thought not, especially since there would have been only the two of us, one girl, one boy, the simple family my mother had long ago dreamed of raising. How different such a life would have been compared to growing up among brothers. She would have eased my way into the world, guiding me as only an older sister could. And as her only brother I would have filled a special place in her heart. Without her I was simply one of four sons. Had she lived I would have been half the equation of a new world.

As I grew older she grew younger, until I thought of her not as my big sister but as the stillborn tragedy of my parents' first year of married life. I was contemplating my own marriage by then and began to appreciate the loss not as a brother but as a father, a loss that seemed to grow more wrenching with time. How could one carry a child for nine months and return home with an empty womb to an empty house? How did one conquer the pain? Where did one find the courage to begin all over again?

When Nancie miscarried in her fourth month the loss my parents had sustained seemed even more crushing than I had once imagined. We had never felt life: there had been no kicking, no heartbeat; it had been too early in the pregnancy for that. We returned home not knowing what it was we had lost beyond the dream of parenthood. But my parents had returned home mourning a daughter who for months had filled them with joyous expectation, stirring

29

just beyond gestation's watery curtain.

In our second pregnancy, a special attachment developed as soon as the invisible limbs of our child began to ripple Nancie's abdomen. Then it became ours in a way the child of no movement had never been, tumbling through that inner space, responding to our voices, to music, to a shift in position. I tried to picture it through my hands, longed to hold what was just barely out of reach. The thought of losing that child now was terrifying; how much more so it would seem after nine months.

I never knew the date of my sister's birth, only the year. But one evening as our pregnancy approached full term I detected an uncharacteristic sadness in my mother's voice. When I pressed her she revealed that on that day, thirty-five years before, my sister had been born. I could not bear to think of the loss just then, so close to our own confinement. Instead I thought of her thirty-fifth birthday, picturing a mature woman with children of her own, a devoted daughter providing my mother with the kind of companionship that only daughters can give. She would have bestowed grandchildren upon my parents long ago; I would have been an uncle. How altered our lives were because a child we never knew had died.

I wanted a daughter, I could make no secret of it. So did Nancie, she because her relationship with her late mother had been so enriching, I because the past seemed to impel it. I had spent my life with brothers, helping to raise the youngest. To my mind there was little mystery in having a son. But to bear a daughter seemed nothing short of miraculous. I dreamed of holding the infant girl my mother had lost, hearing her first cry, raising her to womanhood. How would my mother respond to the news? I wondered.

30

What would she say when we told her we had borne her a granddaughter?

When Nancie was finally delivered of a healthy baby girl, I took my daughter in my arms and wept over her as much in joyous fulfillment of my fondest dreams as in mourning for the sister I had lost. How was it possible that this our most cherished wish had been so quickly realized when that of my parents had been forever foreclosed? I looked down into the searching black eyes of my little girl, heard the piercing voice of her new life, and felt overwhelming relief.

My mother was alone when we called her with the news. Through her tears she repeated, "We have a little girl, we have a little girl." She had been waiting to say that for thirty-five years. Three days later she stood over her granddaughter's crib while Nancie and I looked on. When Elizabeth finally stirred I lifted her gently from sleep and handed her to her grandmother. The tears welled up in all of our eyes then as the past completed itself, and I whispered a silent benediction over my daughter and the soul of my lost sister.

PARENTHOOD

THE PUSHOVER

"She's only three months old," Nancie pleaded in her defense.

"Elizabeth," I said, picking up my crying daughter and holding her a few inches from my face. "If you can't sit here quietly while your parents eat their breakfast, I'm afraid you'll have to spend the rest of the meal upstairs in your crib."

Elizabeth responded to my threat by howling until her face turned red. "Let me hold her," Nancie said. "I can manage with one hand."

"You're lucky your mom is such a pushover," I said, passing Elizabeth to her. "You've already got us wrapped around your little finger, haven't you." Elizabeth smiled, settled comfortably into her mother's lap, and began sucking contentedly on her sleeve while Nancie tried to finish her eggs without spilling them on our daughter's head. "One of these days we're going to have to start disciplining her."

"Oh, Dad," Nancie said as surrogate for Elizabeth, "don't be so tough on me. You know you can't spoil a baby during the first year."

"I don't believe that. Already by three months she knows just how to get us to do her bidding." Elizabeth looked at me and grinned, then went back to her sleeve.

Whenever Elizabeth cried it pained me as much as it did

Nancie, but I lost patience more quickly and was always the first to recommend we start conditioning her. "There's no harm in allowing a baby to cry from time to time," I would argue when all other strategies failed to pacify her. But my more forgiving wife would usually stretch out her hands, take Elizabeth in her arms, and try one more time. Only when that failed, when even the opportunity to nurse did not quiet Elizabeth, would we put her down crying.

It happened rarely, but when it did I usually closed my study door and turned up the stereo to drown out her howls, hoping that she would quickly cry herself to sleep. When the nursery finally fell silent, I always felt vindicated until, tiptoeing into her room, I discovered Nancie, with a conspiratorial grin on her face, holding her grateful daughter. "I couldn't bear it," she would tell me.

"You're lucky your mom is such a pushover," I would respond, relieved by my daughter's sudden comfort, yet concerned that she so thoroughly controlled us.

But then finally last night Elizabeth stretched Nancie's patience to the limit. I was working in my study across the hall when they emerged from the bedroom, Elizabeth crying, Nancie with an uncharacteristic look of frustration on her face. "That's it," she said as she passed my open door. "I've tried everything. It's the crib for you." I applauded her resolve, calling after her as she disappeared into the nursery that at three months it was time we started giving our daughter some direction. Then I closed my door and turned up the stereo.

Five minutes elapsed, or perhaps it was only two, when I lowered the volume and listened. Elizabeth's heartrending sobs showed no sign of abating; she was miserable. How could I sit by and do nothing? She hadn't, after all, resisted *my* efforts at pacification, only Nancie's. Perhaps I should try to calm her. Racked by guilt I leapt from my chair and had my hand on the doorknob when my heart hardened. No, I decided, it was time we began disciplining her, especially since this lesson had been initiated by Nancie. It would have more effect coming from her.

So I turned the volume up again and returned to my work. But then to my astonishment I was standing in the middle of the nursery with my sobbing daughter in my arms, whispering soothing words to her and looking sheepishly at Nancie, who had just discovered my treason.

"I think Dad and I are going out for a walk," Elizabeth said through me. "If anyone calls tell them I'll be back in my crib in half an hour."

"When is it that children start getting spoiled?" Nancie asked, smiling.

"We'll be stricter with the next one," I said, buttoning a sweater on Elizabeth.

A minute later we stepped out into the night where Elizabeth soon fell asleep. When I laid her back in her crib she opened her eyes momentarily, stretched her legs, and then curled up into a deep sleep. I walked into the bedroom and bowed to Nancie's applause. "It was nothing," I said, "nothing that twenty-four hours of continuous attention couldn't accomplish." She smiled knowingly. "By the way," I added, "do you know where my T-shirt is?"

"Which one?" she asked, puzzled.

"The one with PUSHOVER written on the front," I answered.

BABY TALK

A friend of mine believes that all American babies begin life speaking a dialect of Chinese, gradually progressing westward through Russian, Polish, and a host of European tongues until stumbling upon English sometime before their second birthday. Chinese babies, of course, are born with the innate ability to converse in English and gradually work their way east. In her twelfth month, Elizabeth seems poised somewhere west of Rome and east of Gibraltar, possessed of half a dozen words in her mother tongue and an array of Latinate and Iberian-sounding expressions that defy orthography.

Before becoming a parent I used to think that what children said was not nearly as interesting or endearing as what they did. Watching them from afar, I had no idea of the emotional richness of their speech, of their extraordinary articulateness. Now I luxuriate in my daughter's babble, marveling at her tiny voice and its forcefulness. Whenever Nancie calls me at the office I hear Elizabeth in the background filling the house with the sweet music of infant discovery. What did we listen to before she wrote that song? I wonder. It is all I care to hear lately. Indeed, we often record her voice during the day so that we can play it back after she has fallen asleep. We simply cannot get enough of her.

Most mornings Elizabeth talks with her teddy bears for half an hour before calling across the hall to us. Her voice is very different during those *in camera* conversations, softer, more rounded, seemingly less self-conscious. On weekends I lie in bed listening through the wall to her long disquisitions while she turns the pages of her baby books as if reading aloud to the menagerie in her crib. At such moments she seems completely absorbed in the magic that bubbles through her veins, intoxicated by the tuneful eruptions of her soul. No wonder her bears wear a perpetual smile.

My favorite of these sounds reminds me of a popular refrain from the sixties: "du-wah, du-wah." Every time she says it, my wife and I break into song, imitating the backup singers of our youth, dancing in perfect synchronization. I imagine Elizabeth's chubby toddler's body in sequins, standing bowlegged beside two other toddlers, harmonizing their *du-wahs* while Diana Ross croons the melody.

My friend with the theory of innate speech is convinced his daughter is destined to become an accountant. All day long she mutters "debit, debit," to which he automatically responds "credit." He can't help himself; it's reflexive. I understand the mechanism. During the first weeks of Elizabeth's life I used to repeat everything I said to her at least twice, even though she was too young to understand. Since I was not in the habit of repeating myself to adults, I concluded that just as children somehow impel us to raise the pitch of our voices, so they get us to speak in duplicate.

Perhaps we do so because it is difficult coming up with a continuous stream of stimulating subjects while diapering a newborn or spoon-feeding carrot mush to a toddler. These days, whatever Elizabeth says I repeat back to her.

Sometimes we babble at each other for several minutes in a language that only she understands, both of us getting progressively more excited until either she buries her face in my chest and bangs her little fists against my shoulders, giggling, or I kiss her cheeks and toss her into the air to break the tension.

Several of her sounds, however, defy my every attempt at imitation. Produced so far back in her throat, they eliminate all need for vowels. Her favorite goes something like "ldldldld," but with a decidedly Neapolitan lilt, a kind of song that she sings to herself as she goes about the important business of acquainting herself with the world. But when she says "Uh-oh" after dropping her bottle, or "Wowie!" when she succeeds in placing square pegs in square holes, I begin to believe she understands English perfectly.

Indeed, lately I have come to suspect that Elizabeth is toying with me, hoarding a vast store of English in preparation for a great outpouring of thought. This evening as we walked the neighborhood after dinner, a jogger approached. She fastened on him from a distance and moved over to the curb in her slap-footed toddling way, then grabbed my pant leg. "Do you see the runner?" I asked, pointing down the road. She did a little dance of excitement and said "doggie." I said "runner." She said "doggie." I said "doggie." When the runner was only a few steps away, she flapped her hands in an infant wave and said "Hi" in her high-pitched little voice. The runner smiled and waved.

"Where'd you learn that?" I asked, marveling at her first use of the word. Elizabeth repeated it, realizing she was on to something. "Hi yourself," I said, tossing her into the air. "You've been holding out on me, haven't you? What else have you got hidden in that little mind of yours?" She squealed her delight each time I caught her and when finally I put her down, she said "Daddy," with that rising lilt that always melts me.

Whoever said that children should be seen and not heard simply wasn't listening.

MILKMEN

After an interruption of almost fifteen years, milk is beginning to flow back into my life. At the moment it is little more than a trickle but has pretensions of becoming a stream. Perhaps in time it will resemble the great torrent of my youth, that ceaseless flood of calcium and vitamin D that washed before it three meals daily and half a dozen snacks.

Having grown up in a household of four boys whose upper lips were perpetually white (and so, very often, were the tablecloth, our pants, and the floor), I had always taken milk for granted. Every other morning the milkman turned into our driveway, the ice blocks in the back of his truck melting into rivulets that cascaded over the rear bumper as he accelerated up to the house. Jumping down from his high seat, he carried to our kitchen door eight quart bottles in a wire basket, tucking a ninth under his arm along with a dozen eggs and a pound of butter. Two days later, through rain, sleet, and impassable blizzard, he returned with the same order, gathering up the empty bottles from the milk box outside our door.

I never gave a second thought to the quantity of eggs and milk passing through our door during those blissful days of polyunsaturated ignorance, though I do remember hearing my father grumble from time to time that it would have been cheaper to keep a cow and a few chickens. Nevertheless, I think he took a certain pride in the 135 quarts of milk, 180 eggs, and 15 pounds of butter his four sons consumed a month.

In college dairy products all but disappeared from my life. It wasn't that I didn't like milk, just that once I left home I abandoned the habit along with so many other routines of childhood. Then the great arterial age of jogging dawned and medicine began to isolate the fatal effects of high

cholesterol. Whole milk and eggs were singled out as major culprits. Adults were told to eat only one or two eggs a week, to drink only skim milk, and to use margarine instead of butter. I had already made the adjustment, more from sloth than science, finding that margarine spread more easily than butter, that toast required less preparation than eggs, and that orange juice did not sour as quickly as milk. But I shudder to think what a childhood spent consuming daily a quart of milk, one egg, and toast saturated in butter has done to my veins.

After our wedding Nancie and I remained dairy free for years. It simply did not fit into our routine. We rarely ate at home, had no time for breakfast in our rush to the train, and did not drink coffee. When she became pregnant her obstetrician ordained that milk return to our lives and for a few weeks it seemed as if the waxed cardboard containers would find a permanent place in our home. But Nancie could not bear to drink the requisite quart per day; it left her cross-eyed and bloated. So her doctor eventually prescribed calcium pills and once again milk turned sour and then disappeared altogether from our refrigerator.

For the first six months of Elizabeth's life she received all the milk she needed from her mom. But then one memorable afternoon the pediatrician recommended we introduce cereal with whole milk. It only amounted to a tablespoon or two a day, but it was a start. I rushed out to the supermarket in search of the freshest quart and never looked back. Three months later I began bringing home half-gallon containers as Elizabeth weaned herself. The days of discarding sour milk had passed. I could barely keep up with the demand.

And that's when I first thought of having milk delivered. I

hadn't seen a milk truck in the neighborhood since my childhood, and with good reason. When Nancie and I bought our house there were only two aging children on the street, surrounded by elderly couples whose offspring had long since left home. Most of my peers were still too busy with their careers to think about marriage and children. But now, seven years later, fifteen newborns animated the neighborhood and the trend showed little sign of abating. With such a burgeoning market could milkmen be far behind? A quick check of the phone book revealed, to my disappointment, that the industry had not kept pace. Not one was listed.

And then one morning, while driving to the station, I found myself waiting at a light behind an old panel truck with the name and phone number of a dairy scribbled hastily on the rear door. There before me stood the herald of a new age. I jotted the number down and called that afternoon. The man who answered was an independent agent, a pioneering entrepreneur willing to make house calls for little more than the retail price of the items he sold. In addition to milk, butter, and eggs, he was prepared to deliver orange juice, yogurt, bacon, potato chips, and laundry detergent. Throw in disposable diapers, I suggested, and we'll never have to leave the house. His truck couldn't handle the bulk, he said apologetically.

Though the demands of one child hardly warranted it, I harbored a secret yearning to hire that delivery service. I had no intention of becoming a milk drinker myself, but found something irresistible, something warm and comforting in the thought of finding fresh milk on my doorstep. That simple act seemed to make a loving mother of an otherwise indifferent world. Who could fail to be cheered by

45

such a discovery first thing in the morning?

A week later, impelled by that vision, I called to initiate delivery and the next morning stepped out into the light frost of early December to find two bottles of milk and a dozen eggs waiting for me. I hadn't seen glass milk bottles since my childhood. Thrown suddenly back in time by a gesture as simple as bending down to pick up a bottle of milk from the stoop, I felt like my own father. I could not suppress a smile; the milk delighted me.

The blocks of ice have disappeared, replaced by modern refrigeration equipment, but not so the milk box by the door. I get almost as much pleasure placing our empty bottles in it at night as I do discovering fresh milk the next morning. At the moment we receive only five quarts a week, but with children coming back into fashion, who knows? We too may one day need that cow.

A Married Man

After seven years I have grown used to the question, expecting it around the first week in August, just as I am drifting off to sleep. From her side of the bed Nancie whispers through the darkness of a warm night, "Do you still love me?" Clinging to my dream with every ounce of unconsciousness, I mutter back, "Of course I love you. Good night." Unsatisfied, she probes into the shallow recesses of my fast-evaporating sleep, asking, "Are you angry with me?"

By this time I am beginning to experience a vague sense of déjà vu. "No, I'm not angry with you. What makes you ask such a question? I'm crazy about you. But can't we save this for the morning?"

"Then how come we never cuddle anymore? Every time I get near you, you squirm away." Wide awake now, the late night conversations of summers past come flooding back into consciousness along with the day's unbearable heat. "It's almost ninety degrees in here," I remind her. "I'm sticky, short-tempered, and tired. I hate this weather. But I love you—only don't touch me. I can't stand anything pressing against me in this heat."

"We could put on the air conditioner," she generously offers. But neither of us sleeps well beside that chilly roar. Given the choice between a damp sleep and a cool all-night vigil, I always opt for sleep, even if it means keeping to opposite sides of the bed from early June until mid-September.

Perhaps I'm simply getting old and using the heat as an excuse. It is said that men reach their sexual prime at seventeen. I'm almost twice that age and, more telling, glad to be. Or perhaps it's just that summer is no time for warm embraces; a cold shower seems infinitely more enticing on a night when the air itself sticks to your chest.

Before Elizabeth was born I used to joke that our fertility problem had nothing to do with motility rates or blighted ova, it was simply a matter of room temperature. Wait till September, I insisted. You'll be pregnant in no time. It took a couple of Septembers before we got the hang of it, but eventually I was right. Elizabeth's June birth confirmed it.

My earliest memories of our marriage are steeped in heat. The day we wed the temperature hovered in the nineties until well after dark. For the next two weeks scorching weather pursued us from Rome down to Capri and back north to Florence. What sleep we found in our unair-conditioned hotels was fitful until we arrived in Venice. That afternoon the sky turned black, the wind rose, whipping the canals into a white froth, and the temperature dropped twenty degrees. In a room overlooking the Grand Canal, we slept well for the first time as husband and wife, the French windows thrown wide, the long white curtains blowing inward like great tethered pastries, then slowly drifting to the floor. Shortly after midnight I rose to shut out the storm, standing for a moment watching the gondolas bob at their moorings, the black lacquered hulls shim-

mering in the yellow dock light. So, we had finally gotten married, I thought with a smile. After eight years together we had thrown caution to the winds and said, "Let's take a chance." I still don't know what took us so long.

I had not expected to be surprised by marriage after such a lengthy courtship. We had long since laid bare all our shortcomings and fallen into comfortable patterns of accommodation. Yet our new status changed things. For months afterward a guilty pleasure clung to our embraces. I half expected a knock on the door and a stern voice demanding to know whom I had secreted up to my room. Grinning broadly at the ceiling, hands under my head, I would silently remind myself: Our love is legal now. It's more than that, it's a *mitzvah*, a good and blessed deed. That rainy night in Venice I felt the change take hold. Though shouldering new responsibilities I felt somehow taller under the added weight, enjoying the newfound constraints as I did the ring upon my left hand. Life suddenly seemed clearer, less complicated. I had a wife to care for; I was a husband now.

I could not then have imagined the effect that death and children and the simple accumulation of years would have upon us. Some of the changes have been gradual, others instantaneous; some potentially divisive, others unifying. Perhaps because we waited until our mid-twenties to marry, our separate passions have never outstripped our commitment to each other. Warm nights or cold, we share the same bed knowing that just as September follows August, so temporary estrangement will give way to grateful embrace. My hand still seeks Nancie's every night in that moment just before sleep and her lips kiss the air in response.

I thought about all of this the other morning as I awoke shivering beneath a narrow square of bed sheet. In the unexpected cold of a late September morning Nancie had carefully wound the blanket around her, leaving me with barely enough to cover my legs. I rose to shut the windows, then leapt back into bed, burrowing into the tight little cocoon she had made for herself, my teeth chattering, drinking in her heat and suddenly remembering, like a recovered amnesiac, how glorious a warm hug can be on a cold morning. Nancie smiled through her sleep, muttered, "Welcome back, stranger," and fell back asleep with my arms around her.

ANCESTORS

ANCIENT GUILT

Two weeks before my eighty-four-year-old grandfather died he collapsed on the sidewalk near his apartment. Though he suffered no broken bones in the fall, his doctor prescribed a week of bed rest, and for the next few days my grandmother and mother doted over him while he complained good-naturedly that he did not require so much attention. He had no memory of the fall, he told them, and felt fine, just a little sore.

Several days later, however, his abdomen began to swell. He was retaining fluid; his kidneys seemed affected by the fall. The following day he was transferred to a nearby hospital where a battery of tests confirmed his doctor's suspicions. Stroke was mentioned for the first time, not merely as the cause of his kidney failure, but as the probable cause of his fall. How much damage had resulted they could not yet say, nor whether he might suffer additional episodes. But when he began to drift off briefly, appearing perfectly lucid one minute, then suddenly disoriented, they suspected his condition was worsening.

Rapidly his periods of consciousness began to shorten, he slept much of the day, and when he spoke no one understood him. Other organs were beginning to fail. At his age, the doctor said, so precipitous a decline was not uncommon. And in most cases it proved fatal.

He lingered for another week, lying silently in his hospital bed, growing smaller. My parents and grandmother remained by his bedside from early morning until late into the evening, praying for remission, finding renewed hope each time he opened his eyes and squeezed the hand one of them always rested near his weakening fingers. Once or twice he tried to talk, and in those moments his haggard face showed complete awareness, even acceptance, of what was happening to him.

During his final days my grandfather reverted to his native Ladino. First he lost the English he had learned so late in life, then the French and Italian he had acquired during the war, and finally the German of his early years of independence, the years during which he moved to Dresden, made his fortune, married my grandmother, and fathered his only child. Staring up at the black dots in the white acoustical ceiling tile, he mumbled repeatedly about a burro, using words my mother vaguely remembered from her childhood.

He had spoken of the small town of his youth only once to her, but because of the uniqueness of that brief confession she remembered his words. As he lay dying the scene he had long ago described seemed to play repeatedly before his eyes, obliterating the present. When my grandmother tried to reach him in his reverie he did not respond, hearing nothing but the promptings of his own troubled conscience. My mother hung on to his barely audible mutterings for confirmation of her suspicions, believing that he was reliving an old, indelible guilt.

All his life my grandfather had secretly blamed himself for his mother's death, though he had been only three years old at the time. Shortly before she died he had wandered off after an itinerant peddler, a man who trudged through their village every few months with his wares strapped to the ribs of a donkey. Mesmerized by the commotion of the animal and the singsong chant of the salesman, my infant grandfather had followed him out into the countryside where he had been forced to take shelter in a roadside barn when a heavy storm swept over the mountains. The wind rose, the temperature dropped suddenly, and the dusty road turned to mud and rivulets of icy water.

Desperately seeking her lost son, his mother had run out into the rain, knocking on doors, half-mad with fear. Neighbors joined in the search, but by the time he was found she had become so chilled that she took to bed, developed pneumonia, and within weeks died. He blamed himself, he had told his daughter during that one rare moment of confession. And now, in his hospital room, after more than eighty years, he remembered the scene as vividly as if he were just then chasing after the donkey, still lamenting his loss, still seeking forgiveness. Perhaps too he was trying to convince himself one final time that he had been only a child, that someone so young could not be held responsible.

His last night I met my parents in the kitchen as they returned from the hospital shortly after midnight. My grandfather's condition had worsened, they said, so much so that my mother had been reluctant to leave his bedside. Now she stood by the stove, waiting for water to boil while my father leafed listlessly through the mail. They both looked exhausted.

Just as my mother lifted the whistling pot the phone rang. Reflexively she looked up at the clock, then muttered, "Oh my God." My father hurried to her side as she answered. She knew what was coming and said only, "Yes," then listened without responding for several seconds. "When did it happen?" She fell silent again. "No, we will make all the arrangements." When she hung up my father hugged her. She said tearlessly, "I knew we shouldn't have left."

"Shall I drive you back?" he asked. She shook her head and sat down. I poured the tea. When I handed it to her she smiled wanly, rubbing her temples with the fingers of her left hand. Although I had just lost my grandfather, I felt sadness only for her. I did not yet consider the loss my own.

Two days later I helped carry my grandfather to his grave. The heavy oak coffin rested painfully upon my shoulder. For days afterward I felt the impress of his weight in my flesh. As the rabbi recited kaddish I took my mother's hand, fighting back my own tears as she stood silently weeping beside her mother. Then with wet fingers I reached down for a handful of dirt and sprinkled it upon my grandfather's coffin, hoping he had found forgiveness at last.

PASSOVER IN MILAN

In the spring of 1937, having recently fled Nazi Germany, my mother and her parents attended a solemn Passover seder, guests of a Milanese family of Sephardic Jews that traced its ancestry to Inquisitorial Spain and measured its faith by millennia. The patriarch of that ancient household, a white-haired dignitary who commanded the silent respect of an entire community, presided over the ritual meal. Chanting the Hebrew blessings and prayers from his thronelike seat at the head of the crowded table, he recalled, as Jews all over the world were recalling, the biblical tale of slavery and redemption that seemed that year to be speaking not of their past but of their future.

My eleven-year-old mother, awed by her first seder, sat silently beside her mother while her father joined with the other men in muttering an occasional "amen." Until their exile she had only been able to guess at her father's religious devotion. Rarely during her early childhood had he discussed his spiritual beliefs. That he was a devout, even a pious man, that the private promptings of his heart mirrored her own she had always believed, even though she had been raised, for her own protection, in the Lutheranism of her mother rather than in her father's Judaism. For reasons she never understood, he had chosen to live on the fringe of his religious community, eschewing collective worship for more private encounters with God, seemingly indifferent to the rituals of his people if not to the voice that had sustained them for thousands of years. But when Hitler made religion the murderous obsession of a continent, she discovered how thorough was his knowledge of ancient tradition and how deep his identification.

Crowded around the long, formal table that first spring in exile, she had tried to follow the story of the Exodus and its many digressions, but having no Hebrew and little Italian she found herself lost amid the blessings of wine, the dipping of parsley, and the breaking of matzoh. When she turned to her mother for guidance she received only quizzical glances, and her father, seated in a place of honor near the head of the table, was too far away to whisper explanations of the rituals. In the end, the unfamiliar ordeal so exhausted her that she fell asleep against her mother's shoulder while the white-haired patriarch chanted on, blessing yet another cup of wine.

A few months before they were again forced to flee, this time to Paris, my mother and her parents sat again at the table of their Italian friends, prepared once more to mark the anniversary of the Israelites' escape from oppression. That year the gathering was larger, the atmosphere more charged, as if the news of persecution across the border in Austria and Germany and the rumored treaty between Hitler and Mussolini had driven even the most marginal of Jews back to the fold, infusing the past with immediate significance.

The three of them sat together near the middle of the table, my mother between her parents, hoping not only to follow the Italian portions of the seder, but perhaps even some of the Hebrew with her father's guidance. Once again the family patriarch sat stiff backed in the great carved chair at the head of the table, his oldest son by his side. In the intervening year the old man had aged greatly, his once awesome appearance now frail, his steely blue eyes clouded and watery. My mother noticed several of the guests exchanging worried glances as he raised the wine-stained Haggadah and recited the first blessing in a thin and halting voice, his spotted hands trembling.

They all had come seeking comfort and renewed strength in the midst of their feverish uncertainties, only to find that the pillar of their community had begun to crumble under the accumulated weight of old age and rising sorrow. His voice barely reached my mother at the middle of the table. Those at the far end of the room could not follow. And then after only a few minutes he faltered. For a moment his eyes seemed to read on in silence; then they closed. His son placed a hand on his forearm and asked if he was well enough to continue. The old man shook his head imperceptibly, laid the Haggadah upon his plate, and then with help rose from the table and left the room.

Other men of stature in the community sat at the table, men who had openly and generously supported the Jewish institutions of Milan. In the patriarch's absence they turned to each other, seeking someone confident enough with the ancient tongue to assume the vacant seat at the head of the table and continue the seder. But one by one they declined, citing either poor vision or imperfectly remembered Hebrew.

Finally they turned to my grandfather. Though decades had passed since he last entered a synagogue, years in which he had neither practiced the rituals nor celebrated the festivals of his faith, he rose and to my mother's astonishment assumed the patriarch's seat. His silent, intensely private devotion was no less powerful for having been so long concealed, she realized. Indeed, as he chanted the ancient Hebrew of his forefathers, his faith sparkled with such incandescence that my mother sat in awe, discovering him as if for the first time as he led the embattled Jewish community of Milan out of Egypt.

RETURN TO DRESDEN

They traveled alone, mother and daughter, returning to the city that had first nurtured and then banished them. In the forty years since their exile, much had changed. The famous central district with its rococo cathedrals and Renaissance palaces had been destroyed by Allied bombs, tens of thousands had perished, a Communist regime had taken power. But the house to which my newly married grandmother had moved in 1921, and in which my mother had been born, still stood according to their last surviving contact in Dresden. It alone remained of all that had been their lives, it and perhaps the graves of my grandmother's parents. The rest, they knew as they boarded the train in Frankfurt for the long trip east, had perished in the great conflagration, victim of Hitler, Stalin, or simply of time.

For years they had spoken of making that journey back into their past, my grandmother to pay one final visit to her ancestral home, my mother to test the accuracy of childhood memories, to see just once with adult eyes what she had known only as a child. Not until the death of my grandfather did they finalize their plans, propelled by a new urgency. For in his deeply grieved absence they sought not merely to commune with a warmly remembered past, but to make contact with his spirit, to revisit the landmarks that had circumscribed the happiest years of his life and theirs, forgetting, perhaps for a moment, that forty years of exile had intervened, that the land of their birth, once so beloved, had become so alien, so repellent.

Whenever my grandmother talked about Dresden, she recalled the good years, the first decades of this century when, as the youngest of six children, she had enjoyed all the privileges of an adored last child. She spoke also of the twenties, the early years of her marriage, years of abundance, rising social and political influence, and the birth of her daughter. And she remembered the early thirties, before Hitler, when the city had seemed her private jewel, when no door had been closed to her. But then it all crumbled. Overnight they had become fugitives, forced to flee across the Alps into Italy. At first my grandmother's Lutheranism and the baptism of her daughter protected them. But when the blood hatred of her kinsmen intensified against her Jewish husband none of them were safe.

So they sold what little they could of their treasured belongings and escaped to Milan, where for two years they attempted to rebuild their lives, learning a new language, adjusting to new customs. Then Mussolini declared his sympathy with Hitler's racial laws and once more they fled, this time to Paris. Through a combination of well-placed friends and false papers, they survived the war, living in the shadow of the Gestapo, never knowing when a knock on the door or a sudden street search might mean deportation and death.

At war's end my mother converted to the Judaism of her father, married a childhood friend, a German Jewish refugee from Berlin, and sailed for New York. Fifteen years later her parents followed, determined to spend the last years of their lives near their only child. By that time Dresden had disappeared behind an iron curtain of silence. Their only remaining contact, the aging daughter of a former business associate, wrote once a year to say that since the war nothing was the same. Whenever my mother wrote back she had the feeling she was corresponding with ashes.

Six years after my grandfather's death, my mother and grandmother finally returned to Germany. The first leg of their pilgrimage was the easiest, as they knew it would be. Paris was warm and welcoming, their friends still numerous, especially those of the postwar years. The adjustment was instantaneous, even the language returned to them with ease. When they stood outside the apartment that had harbored them during the war and after, it seemed to my grandmother as if she need only reach into her purse for the house key to reenter a life still so fresh in her mind. Paris had been good to them.

But not so Milan. Death had taken a great toll, leaving behind only a handful of old friends. The reunion was little more than a somber review of loss and encroaching feebleness. Perhaps the worsening weather was to blame; perhaps too the knowledge that their next and final destination was to be the most wrenching.

The fall rains had arrived by the time they boarded a plane for the flight to Frankfurt and continued with little interruption for the next week. The following day as their train began the long ride eastward, the windows became mirrors in the sudden darkness of violent storms. They rode much of the way in silence, my grandmother drifting in and out of sleep, exhausted by anticipation, my mother watching the sodden landscape streak by, anxious about crossing to the other side. When they reached the border, jackbooted officials searched their baggage and confiscated two French magazines. Until they arrived in Dresden they spoke in whispers, worrying about their safety, wondering whether they should turn back. At moments it felt as if they were reliving the nightmare of forty years ago, inexplicably returning to the fire. When the train finally reached its destination, they hesitated, unwilling to relinquish the security and comfort of their compartment for the cold and rainy city that no longer remembered them, a city they no longer recognized. They felt orphaned, lost.

The Dresden they had known, opulent and familial, had vanished, taking with it the countless relatives and friends that had populated their past. In its place stood a dour, undistinguished matrix of glass and steel, as joyless as the expressions of the people they encountered, as lifeless as the bombed-out hulk of the Hof Kirche, hanging black and mutilated on the banks of the Elbe, a gruesome reminder of a former glory and its brutal eclipse. This was not the city they had left; it was an imposter.

For seven days they wandered like pilgrims in search of a lost shrine. The woman my mother had continued to correspond with for forty years guided them through the open squares, pointing to faceless office buildings and recalling the ancient stones that had once graced those streets. After so many years it was becoming difficult to keep the old images alive, she told them sadly. Few remained who could do so from memory.

But the outskirts of the city had not been bombed, she assured them, not their neighborhood anyway. The house of my mother's birth was still intact. And so, after they had toured the rest of the city, they rode out in a cab, my mother and grandmother locking nervous hands as they approached the site of so much remembered happiness. From a distance it appeared unchanged, the great iron gate freshly painted, the house appearing almost exactly as they had left it so many years before. For a moment it seemed as if it had all been a terrible mistake, a bad dream. There it stood awaiting their return, welcoming them as though they had never left, as though Hitler had never declared an end to the Jews and their once-beloved kinsmen had not joined him in the purge.

But as they approached the great gate of the stately stone house, another jackbooted guard stopped them. State property, he announced. No entry. Retrieving her detested and half-forgotten German, my mother explained that the house had once been theirs, that the Nazis had expropriated it, that they had traveled thousands of miles to walk one last time through its rooms. They would disturb no one. He refused. Could they merely walk to the front door and peer through the glass? my mother asked, her anger rising. He remained obdurate; they could get no closer than the street, no exceptions. In bitter frustration they turned away from their home for the last time, their reasons for fleeing forty years ago suddenly so clear. In the interim one hostile regime had replaced another. The bleakness had remained. They could not wait to leave that poisoned land.

On their final day they drove to the cemetery in the hope of finding the graves of my grandmother's parents. She had not visited the site since the early thirties and was at a loss how to proceed once they passed through the front gate. But my mother, who as a little girl of six had been present at the burial of her grandmother, remembered those neatly manicured lawns and footpaths. Long after the rest of the city had faded from memory, that image remained with her. And miraculously, relying upon her childhood vision, she rediscovered the graves.

Everything else in their lives had changed; only the dead remained undisturbed, bearing silent testimony to an ancient allegiance. And for a moment, as they stood together over their past, the intervening years, years of long exile and sorrow, vanished and they were once again the children of their beloved city and of their confiscated dreams.

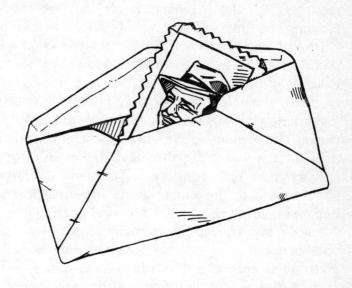

A Childless Grandfather

While Nancie and Elizabeth napped in the living room, I sat in the kitchen with Nancie's eighty-seven-year-old grandfather, sorting through pictures of his family. The oldest photos, torn and stained victims of a century of abuse, had been rescued from pogroms and neglect, preserved by him in a tattered envelope stored in the top drawer of his bureau. Most of the pictures bore some identifying mark on the back: a hastily scribbled name, a date, and sometimes a brief message. But the oldest, two sepia portraits taken in Russia, were unmarked. He alone could breathe life back into the stiff poses of his sunken-eyed father and dour-faced mother. He alone remained of the generation that remembered them and that age of violent dislocation.

He had long ago chosen 1896 as the year of his birth but had no legal record of the event. Neither did he know the exact ages of his long-dead brothers and sisters. But when he sorted through photos of them, putting on thick glasses and taking up a large magnifying glass to make the faded images visible to his aged eyes, he spoke of them as though their presence were palpable. Then he would range over a century and a half of history and suddenly the distant and impersonal past, the suffering and hope that had brought him and millions of others to America, came to life.

Among his collection were many recent photos as well, color snapshots of nieces, nephews, grandnieces, and even a great-grandnephew, each of whom he identified in the loud voice of the hearing impaired, passing from generation to generation with the total if halting recall of a devoted uncle. He loved his collection for the memories they evoked, and his visitors for the opportunity they provided to recall those memories.

His first marriage had been childless and after his wife's death he had remained a widower for decades. During those solitary years he had devoted himself to the children of his brothers and sisters, adding their twentieth-century offspring in Israel and America to his photo collection of nineteenth-century Russia. Alone in his tiny West Side apartment, he held together the disparate strands of his far-flung family while the nieces and nephews had children and grandchildren. Though they lost touch with each other they never lost touch with him. The newborn, the recently graduated, the just married were dutifully reported in letters and photos; and whenever any relative visited he would amble off to his dresser, remove the thick envelope, and draw the photos out one by one, relating their stories in detail, savoring his family.

Then, at the age of seventy-five, he married Nancie's grandmother and began to accumulate photos of his new family with the same devotion he showed his nieces and nephews, adding them to the same tattered envelope. Among them was a photo of his latest grandchild, Elizabeth, which he showed me with special fondness. Those who were dear to his wife were instantly dear to him. He welcomed us into his heart without trial or reservation, quickly becoming the grandfather of us all. Nature had denied him children, yet he who had never been a father had become the great-grandfather of our child. Although a link was missing, the chain remained unbroken, and we felt as enriched by his past as he felt by our future.

HOME ECONOMICS

DECIPHERING THE SUPERMARKET

For years I rarely set foot inside our local supermarket, doing so only under duress. It was a place, it seemed to me, for frazzled young mothers and fragile old widows, for the atavists who still did their own cooking, not for young professionals who worshipped raw fish and corned beef sandwiches. And since both Nancie and I believed with religious conviction that nothing should take longer to prepare than it did to eat, and since we rarely spent longer than ten minutes at the table, we had little use for our local grocery.

Occasionally, when the deli ran out of eggs or orange juice I would venture across the street prepared to be intimidated by the supermarket's long rows, wondering how it was that others seemed to negotiate them with such confidence. What did people do with all that food? I wondered. Not that I was a complete culinary illiterate; I understood produce, could peel carrots, slice peppers, dice mushrooms, and pick a decent head of lettuce. And I knew my way around tuna fish, ice cream, and snack food. But the plethora of pasta, the menagerie of meat, fish, and fowl, the endless array of milk products, grains, and exotic vegetables—these belonged to a realm that only the cognoscenti of the kitchen understood.

And then suddenly something happened. It began with flour and slowly grew to encompass more than half the rows of my supermarket. A dilettante at heart, I awoke one Saturday and decided for the sake of my newborn child and those yet to come that I needed to learn to bake bread in the event of some global catastrophe. How could I march through life self-confidently providing for my family if every step of the way I relied on the baked goods of others?

A few years before I had decided just as precipitously that a man should not go to his grave never having played the clarinet. Two years of Saturday morning lessons ensued until the desire for sleep and the realization that I was without any talent whatsoever impelled me to hang up my reed.

Perhaps it was the void left behind by the interruption of those lessons that triggered my search for new realms to conquer, for suddenly that Saturday morning I found myself in the local library thumbing through cookbooks (we had none at home) and scribbling directions and ingredients on a scrap of paper while visions of croissants and cracked wheat danced in my head.

Then for the first time the supermarket worked for me. It was not meant to be an archive of archaic edibles, a museum of slow foods in a high-tech era, but a resource for us all—the most democratic of institutions. So I took my list, the first in my life that didn't include Coke, potato chips, or half a pound of cole slaw, and marched through the automatic doors prepared to conquer marketing.

I had a vague memory of stumbling upon most of the needed ingredients, having once accidentally strayed from my usual rows: toilet paper, soft drinks, and Pop Tarts. But now as I went in search, my heart beating with the excitement of a child on an egg hunt, I found nothing but instant waffles. At the sight of them my gorge rose: imagine eating ready-made frozen waffles when one could make them oneself out of pure and wholesome ingredients. Was that me talking? I wondered. Had I so quickly renounced my profligate past and become a reformed fast-food junkie, full of pieties about the evils of haste? Beatific imaginings of white chef's hats, gleaming stainless steel kitchens, and adoring guests stunned into openmouthed awe by my cooking suddenly filled my thoughts.

With the help of two checkout girls and the manager (I was reluctant to ask the same person twice and appear a total novice) I located everything on my list and then waited proudly at the checkout line, hoping that the woman behind me would notice my five-pound bag of flour and initiate a discussion on the virtues of bleached versus un-bleached. When she said nothing I looked to the checkout girl for at least a fleeting expression of admiration for my pioneering spirit, my return to basics, my courage: I had discovered that bread could be baked, certainly a realization worthy of praise. But all I got was a register receipt and the query, "One bag or two?" Yet even that thrilled me. I had never walked out of the supermarket before with enough groceries to warrant a second bag. Hugging them to my chest, I headed for the car, smiling broadly, ready to conquer the world of baking.

Perhaps if my first loaf had approximated bread in texture or taste I might have declared baking conquered and moved on to other noble endeavors like oil painting. But the misshapen, tasteless mound of charred crust and gritty dough was even rejected by the birds when I left it on the back patio—and this in the middle of winter. The following

Saturday, however, my efforts were rewarded with something that worked well as croutons. I was getting there, and in the process discovering the joys of transforming the kitchen into a battlefield, bowls balanced precariously in the sink; flour, sugar, and honey covering every surface; wooden spoons and vinyl spatulas stuck to the counter.

Soon thereafter I opened my cookbook accidentally to fish, chanced upon a photo of sole almondine, and strode into the living room to announce that the delicacies of expensive Manhattan restaurants were now within our grasp. I had broken the code, deciphered the hieroglyphics of cuisine, mastered the language of pots and pans, and could now prepare a gourmet meal. Nancie smiled benignly; she always admired enthusiasm. That Saturday I rose early, consulted my steadily growing library of cookbooks, made my list, and marched off to the supermarket in pursuit of glory. And then suddenly the scales fell from my eyes and I saw those long shelves for what they truly were: an artist's palette, the means to an infinite variety of creative ends. The realization flooded my soul with celestial light as I sailed along the rows gathering foods to my bosom, blessing them, the market, and myself.

I have not been the same since that day. Frankly, the almondine was mediocre, overcooked and underseasoned, but there was no turning back. From that moment on cooking ceased to be a weekend sport and became instead a nightly passion. There was a time when Nancie and I ate out six nights a week and on the seventh ordered in pizza. But since my rebirth we have hardly eaten at another table. Every night on my way home from work I stop at the market and wander along the rows in search of inspiration, anticipating the day when I shall transmit the secrets of this noble tradition to my children. For, in truth, the supermarket is a holy place, a shrine, a temple that nourishes the spirit, and I have become one of its most ardent disciples.

COLLECTING CHAIRS

During the last few years our basement has become the final resting place for dozens of chairs: white ones, green ones, brown ones; desk chairs, bridge chairs, kitchen chairs; bar stools, chaise longues, and even a disjointed recliner. I once thought myself beneficent in offering them to the college-bound children of friends and neighbors. Their gracious thanks long deceived me into believing that one bright day they would arrive with station wagons and relieve the congestion below stairs. But semesters passed and then graduations and still the chairs remained piled on each other, a fertile matrix of wooden legs and spider webs. It is easier, it seems, to accumulate chairs than to divest oneself of them, even when the offering price is a very affordable gratis.

One wet spring afternoon, after a long absence from the basement, I returned in search of a cache of old letters. Chairs now occupied every corner—good, strong, well-upholstered chairs. What was it about them that evoked such indifference? They were comfortable, practical, even endearing, and all in good repair. Yet no one seemed to want them. Given enough rooms, I would have returned them all to service. But our house is small and our chairs many.

Forgetting my original purpose, I turned a long-forgotten armchair upright and sat down, recalling the apartment it had served so many years before. That single room off campus furnished from my parents' basement and the basements of their friends had marked the beginning of my independence. I had gladly accepted those handouts, pledging to follow the magnanimous example of my parents'

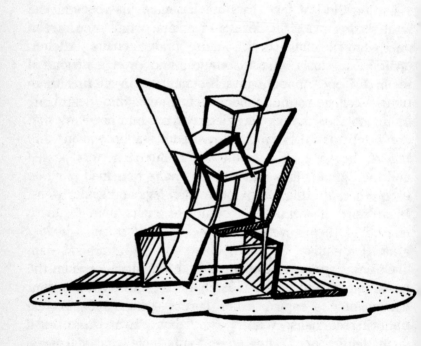

generation as soon as I had established a basement of my own. But a basement and the best of intentions cannot disseminate excess chairs to an indifferent world. I was born too late. The children of my friends prefer to sit on the floor.

When Nancie caught me at the top of the stairs with a chair under each arm she smiled, kissed my cheek, and sent me back down. We simply have no room for any more chairs upstairs. Times change and the dreams of one generation become the jokes of another. I once imagined myself the generous provider of furnished apartments for young people just starting out; now I feel like an old fool attempting to tender Confederate currency. I do not offer to part with such old friends lightly. But no one seems to appreciate either the profundity of my offer or the value of my chairs. So for the time being they will simply have to remain with us, aging companions, each a comfortable reminder of some cherished phase of a sweet life.

WASHED UP

I had just put Elizabeth down for her afternoon nap, intending to spend an hour reading in the garden, when the washing machine sprang a leak. Like most incompetent home owners, I enjoy butchering simple mechanical chores, transforming leaking toilets into flooded bathrooms. But I scrupulously avoid all malfunctioning electrical appliances. After one year of high school chemistry, two of physics, and seven years of changing my own light bulbs, I still do not know the difference between a volt, a watt, and an amp. I probably would have felt right at home in the first half of the nineteenth century, sometime before the industrial revolution began playing under lights. I understand steam and internal combustion, but generally leave alternating current to my electrician.

When I traced the narrow stream of water to the back of the washing machine, however, I suspected a mechanical rather than an electrical mishap. And since I'm as handy as the next guy when it comes to replacing rubber hoses, I wrestled the ageless steel-and-enamel machine away from the wall, fumbled about in the half-light for the drip, and discovered that it came not from a hose at all but from somewhere deep within the incomprehensible electronic bowels of the thing. Knowing my limits, I shoved the unit back against the wall and reached for a phone book.

But who was I to call? I did not even know the make of the machine, not to mention the year or model. It looked old, 1950s old, which is to say it had no plastic parts, the corners were rounded, and it weighed three times more than a comparable up-to-date model. When I moved into the house and found it standing beside the basement sink I assumed that, like the other appliances left behind, it was purely decorative. But a turn of the controls proved otherwise. Grateful during that season of bottomless expenses for even token relief, I pressed it into service. Seven years later it was still spinning flawlessly (which is to say that no more than half a dozen socks disappeared a year), while my new dryer had already cost me $140 in service calls.

Little that touches our lives today is supposed to remain with us for the duration of the journey. Cars, homes, spouses, children—all come with a limited warranty. When the ice maker fails and the serviceman offers to repair it for $218 or replace the entire refrigerator for $395, we shrug and opt for the new. After all, if a $15,000 car cannot be expected to give full value after two years, how can we complain when a refrigerator requires replacement after three? There is security in newness: a one-year warranty, the availability of parts, the serviceman's familiarity with the equipment. Those who fail to stay current must pay the price. After two or three years you're on your own.

So, who was I to call about repairing something that had probably long since been classified as unserviceable? On a hunch I tried a well-known manufacturer and discovered that for $25 they would send a man to look over the problem and tell me whether or not he could repair it. I knew those so-called repairmen. Riding around in authentic-looking service trucks, they have but one purpose in life: to sell you new equipment. No doubt he would show up in overalls, shine a flashlight into the machine, flip through his repair manual and price list, tap a few numbers into a pocket calculator, and then announce with a perfectly straight face that for nearly the price of a new machine he could make the needed repair—provided he could still get the parts. Of course, his efforts were guaranteed only ninety days. A new machine carried a one-year warranty. It might take six weeks to repair the old. He could have a new machine installed in five working days. It was my choice, of course, but he knew what he would do.

I knew the routine. I was a sitting duck, a postindustrial patsy, but what choice did I have? So I scheduled the service call and resigned myself to an expenditure of $25 for the privilege of being told that my problem was not a small leak in the basement but a large hole in my pocket. I spent the next hour trying to read, stewing about the human condition, then suddenly grew tired of being victimized by machinery and marched back down to the basement to do battle with my incompetence.

Yanking the washer away from the wall, I reached inside to the site of the leak and nearly electrocuted myself. Wisdom dictated retreat, but the prospect of spending $400 helped to concentrate my energies and marshal my courage. Once more I approached the machine, pulled the plug, and dove in with both hands, emerging a sweaty hour later

holding the leaky culprit in my blackened, greasy fingers, poised upon the dawn of a new age of self-sufficiency.

When I cancelled the $25 house call, I thought I detected a note of disappointment in the dispatcher's voice. But when I asked to speak to the parts department her tone brightened. The clerk asked for the model and make, which I had discovered on a plate inside the washer. Two minutes later I heard him whistle. "That machine's older than I am." His tone seemed faintly censorious, as if there was something shameful if not cruel in keeping such an aged machine in service. "Built in nineteen fifty-nine."

"Can I still get parts?" I asked sheepishly.

"That all depends," he replied. "What do you need?"

He might as well have asked me to describe the process of nuclear fusion. I twittered for a moment, looking for the right words, then said, "It comes from the back where the hoses screw in."

"The mixing valve?" he asked.

"If you say so."

"Any number on it?"

I read several faded digits and then waited while he flipped through his catalogue. "Probably a five-eight-one-two-six," he decided.

"Are you sure?"

"I could be wrong. Anyway, I don't have it in stock. It'll cost you twenty-two ninety-five plus tax. Want to order it?"

Something told me to proceed with caution, it was going too well. Surely a twenty-five-year-old part could not be so easily replaced.

"How about if I come down and show you what I'm holding before we order anything?"

"Suit yourself. We close at five."

The clerk who eventually helped me knew nothing about my earlier phone conversation. He flipped through his catalogue and came up with an entirely different part number. When I mentioned 58126 he shrugged, not as if to say it was incorrect, just somehow irrelevant. I looked at the picture, saw a vague resemblance to the part I held in my hand, and told him to proceed.

"It's eleven ninety-five plus tax," he said.

The longer I stayed in the repair business the less it was costing me. I could barely contain my delight. I was beating them at their own game. "How long till it comes in?"

"Ten days if they have it, otherwise three weeks."

"Three weeks for what?"

"To let you know they don't make it anymore."

"Then what?"

"You're outa luck."

In other words, for want of a twelve-dollar part I would end up having to buy a new machine after all. So my thrill of triumph had been premature. They were cagier than I thought. I had slipped through the first line of defense, the repairman, only to be pinned down by the more cleverly disguised second line: parts. Something told me my destiny had already been sealed. Still I ordered the valve and returned home, spirits deflated, sensing doom.

That night I dreamed I was held prisoner by a commercial laundry, coerced into spending nearly as much to clean my shirts and socks as I would have spent to buy a new machine. Every time I called the parts department they put me on hold, forcing me to listen to synthesized renditions of "Michelle" and the theme from *Chariots of Fire* until I hung up in frustration. In an overstarched rage I wrote threatening letters promising legal action. Then suddenly the valve arrived, leering at me in all its plastic incompatibility. Of course it did not fit. They knew all along it wouldn't, intending to teach me a lesson for keeping my old washer in service for so long. It was un-American, unethical. Let him squirm a little, they figured. When we finally rescue him with our most expensive model, he'll be willing to pay anything.

Then suddenly, my dream presented me with a gleaming new washing machine, its gold-edged warranty taped inside the lid. "Any problems," the installer boasted, "just give us a call." He eyed my seven-year-old dryer with a reproachful air. I obviously had not learned my lesson. "Look's like that baby's getting on," he said almost threateningly, jotting down something in his appointment book. "Have you seen our new model?"

"This one still works fine," I said meekly.

"Gave you a problem last year, didn't it? Seems to me you've already thrown enough money after this tired old box, money that might better have been put toward a brand-new one. If I were you, I'd come down to the showroom this afternoon."

"Perhaps I will," I lied, trying to lead him to the stairs.

"It's a free country, of course. But a man's got an obligation to his family and friends, to his community, to the nation. I know what most good folks would do."

I never could tolerate flag-waving speeches, awake or asleep. This one shattered my dream and propelled me into consciousness just as the sun was rising on the second day of my new vocation. I spent the afternoon pricing washing machines in preparation for the inevitable.

And then, to my astonishment, the valve arrived. My heart racing, I marched down to the basement, trying not to think about success until it was achieved, envisioning screws stripping, wires fizzling, and headlines reading: MAN KILLS WASHING MACHINE, PLEADS INSANITY—SAYS HE WAS CRAZY TO EVER ATTEMPT HIS OWN REPAIRS. But fifteen minutes later, valve in place, the washer sat back against the wall quietly filling with warm water.

"Beginner's luck," I muttered in disbelief, watching it spin. When it finally fell silent at the end of the cycle, I patted its side. "Hang in there," I said. "We old guys have to stick together."

RAISING TWINS

EXPECTING TWINS

"I tried for eleven years to have a child," Marilyn said as we ringed the table introducing ourselves, "saw dozens of specialists, underwent nine operations, and finally tried in vitro fertilization—all without success. The rest is history."

The rest, for those of us who could see her, was unmistakable: She was pregnant, extremely pregnant, ecstatically pregnant—and with twins!

"Do you know what you're having?" the woman beside her asked.

When Marilyn answered, "A boy and a girl," the room burst into applause.

Fifteen of the women in that room had already given birth, five, including Nancie, were approaching delivery. As the introductions continued, I whispered to her, "I can't believe we're sitting here." Like the others, we felt the need to talk about the future, not because we did not know what to expect from parenthood—most of us already had children at home—but because we were all expecting twins, an unsettling prospect at any stage of child rearing.

"My boys are three and a half and I love them dearly," Angela prefaced, "but they are busting my chops." The seasoned mothers laughed knowingly, the expectant ones nervously. "I didn't sleep for the first year, and I haven't stopped running since. If I can make it to kindergarten, I think I'll survive until college, but some days I have my doubts. Those are the days I begin to feel a certain sympathy with celibacy." The same knowing laughter circled the table.

I had never given so much as a passing thought to the notion that I might someday father twins. Leaping from an airplane seemed only slightly more hazardous and infinitely less unreasonable. So when Nancie called one morning during her third month of pregnancy to say that her obstetrician, finding her unusually large for that stage of gestation, was sending her for an unscheduled sonogram, I did not immediately conclude the obvious; I worried rather that something had gone terribly wrong, that we were about to suffer another miscarriage.

When, an hour later, she asked in classic fashion if I was sitting down, I knew from the almost palpable laughter in her voice that not only was she fine, but that we had just entered a region few parents ever explore—twindom. "God only grants twins to special parents," her obstetrician had declared in conveying the news. Before I had a chance to reflect on our singular grace, she reminded me that he was the father of twin boys.

Joanna leaned forward into the table and introduced herself as insane. "I already have a nineteen-year-old daughter and a three-year-old son. What do I need two more children for, and at my age? Everyone's going to think these kids belong to my daughter, that I've adopted her illegitimate children."

"At least you've got built-in baby-sitting," one of the other mothers added.

"Just when I need her," Joanna lamented, "she's leaving for college. I wish I could join her."

"You're gonna need help," the discussion leader, a seasoned veteran, announced to the expectant among us. "Two hands are not enough, not in the beginning. If you can afford to pay someone, great, if not, don't turn down your mother or your mother-in-law when they offer to spend a few weeks helping out, even if you can't stand to be with them. If possible, convince your husband to take a leave of absence. Twins are a handful."

Twins! After the initial shock wore off, I staggered through the office spreading the news, eliciting looks of sympathy and awe. The men uniformly wished me good luck with a tone of gratitude that declared, "Better you than me." The women, more varied in their response, either moaned, "Your poor wife," or announced, "I always wanted twins." Until that moment I had thought multiple births a blessing less envied than endured.

A few friends thought we were terribly clever to get our childbearing over so quickly. When I tried to explain that I was in no rush to dismantle the crib, they looked at me as if I had overdosed on infant formula. "Aren't three enough?"

"It's not the number," I emphasized, "but the interval from first to last. I don't want all my children leaving the house at once. I'd rather see them trickle away gradually."

Some merely shrugged; a few insisted, "You'll change your tune when they reach adolescence." The only reason parents put up with the exorbitant costs of college, they explained, is that after eighteen years of mayhem, one is willing to pay almost any price for a little privacy, a little peace and quiet, a little sanity.

The night we learned our lives were to be forever altered, Nancie and I sat in the dining room watching Elizabeth smear dinner diagonally across her bib. "Do you realize there are going to be three high chairs in this room?" Nancie pointed out.

"Three car seats," I added.

"Two cribs."

"A double stroller."

"Trainloads of disposable diapers."

"Truckloads of baby food."

"One will always be hungry."

"One will always be crying."

"We'll never sleep."

"We'll never go anywhere. Can you imagine trying to dress three children and get them out in time for anything? I can barely manage one. How are we going to survive?"

Elizabeth knocked her milk onto the floor. "Do you remember the day we learned you were pregnant with her?" I reflected, grabbing a sponge. We had run through the city telling strangers our good news, calling everyone we could think of, toasting our good fortune. Twins are born under a very different emotional constellation.

"There is no way to prepare to be the parents of twins," the discussion leader offered in response to one expectant mother's confession of self-doubt. "There's really nothing else like it. The only way to learn is by doing." Seeing the concern on our faces, she hastily added, "Don't be frightened by all our horror stories; twins are the most rewarding experience in the world."

The other mothers quickly echoed her enthusiasm, the mood shifted, the prospect brightened. After hearing my worst fears reflected in the experiences of others, I was grateful for the encouragement.

But as the meeting ended I glanced down the long table at these, God's chosen parents, and asked, "Have any of you had children after your twins?"

The fifteen seasoned mothers looked at each other and laughed. None had.

TWINS: THE REALITY

December 7

I discovered last night why one rarely encounters highly pregnant women at cocktail parties, especially women carrying twins: they can't reach the hors d'oeuvres. It took Nancie half an hour just to cross the crowded living room. She could not simply turn sideways like the rest of us and squeeze past everyone locked in cocktail conversation. She is wider now from back to front than from side to side. So at each impasse she had to wait for someone to notice her condition and move aside—*substantially* aside. As they did, the guests reacted with a mixture of awe and sympathy: "You poor woman, what are you doing on your feet?" Several even offered to run interference.

But as she approached the canapés a certain blind indifference began to prevail. Moving laterally as they fed, the hungriest guests failed to notice or make room for her. Had I not muscled my way in, she might have starved. "A cocktail party is no place for a pregnant woman," I whispered, leading her and a full plate to safety.

I adore her shape. It not only defies description, it defies gravity. She can no longer reach the kitchen faucet or tie her own shoes. How does a woman carrying so much weight remain upright? In truth, she doesn't. The burden of two near-term infants is so great that she has spent the better part of her ninth month in bed, searching in vain for a comfortable position. Maternity gowns are the only clothes that fit her, great tentlike affairs that could double as bedspreads or infield tarps.

Surprisingly, she has gained less than she did carrying Elizabeth. Her abdomen is so crowded that eating has ceased to be a pleasure. So in the absence of outside resources, the little cannibals have taken to living off her flesh, visibly thinning her face and arms. She will emerge from this ordeal lighter than she began—the one benefit, she says, of trial by twins.

Along with eating, sitting, and breathing, sleeping has also become impossible. The babies kick all night, convert even the blandest foods into hydrochloric heartburn, and have prompted the release of hormones that make her skin itch. I often wake in darkness to the sound of running water: at three in the morning Nancie is bathing. The buoyancy and warmth provide some measure of relief, but the effects are short-lived. Minutes after returning to bed she begins to moan, "Enough already! I'm ready to meet these kids."

Is she? Am I? I'm not sure that anyone can ever be fully prepared for twins. I shudder at the thought of trying to pacify two crying infants in the middle of the night, of changing endless diapers, of cleaning mountains of laundry. How do two adults coerce three small children into a car? What car is big enough for the five of us and all the attendant paraphernalia newborns require? When will Nancie and I ever have time for each other or for ourselves? The prospect of twin boys terrifies me. They'll tear the house apart. Girls seem far more manageable, though mixed doubles would be ideal.

December 11

What is more incongruous than a highly pregnant woman at a cocktail party? That same woman scaling a nearly vertical stepladder into a dark attic on a subfreezing night.

In a spasm of delayed nesting—she's due any moment—Nancie suddenly decided this evening to search for a missing box of baby clothes. With my head and hands positioned beneath her buttocks, she rose slowly but resolutely skyward, pausing every few steps to catch her breath, which crystallized in the light of the bare overhead bulb. If someone had told me while Nancie lay moaning in bed this morning, suffering intermittent contractions, that she would have the strength not merely to sit up this evening, but to probe into the darkest recesses of our attic, I would have laughed the sardonic chuckle of one who has lived with a semi-invalid for three months. Yet there she was, flashlight in hand, searching for the tiny clothes that Elizabeth relinquished an eternity ago. The quest brought color to her cheeks. That brief journey under the eaves was the closest she's come in weeks to spending a night out.

December 14

We did it! Or rather, Nancie did it. Two beautiful babies late this afternoon. When Elizabeth was born it was just the two of us, our obstetrician, and a nurse. The birth of twins is considerably less intimate. All told, there were nine of us squeezed into the operating theater: two obstetricians, one pediatrician, the anesthesiologist, three nurses, and us. By the time it was all over that number had risen magically to eleven without anyone using the door.

Our obstetrician took command from a low stool at Nancie's feet, calmly directing his troops as she labored loudly. His assistant, a burly, soft-spoken man, stationed himself at Nancie's side, his fingers on her abdomen, sensing each contraction and helping her to push.

At 5:29 the head of our first twin emerged from darkness with the umbilical cord wrapped around its neck. The obstetrician eased one shoulder out, unwound the cord, then continued to guide our child into this world, announcing, "It's a boy." My first feelings were mixed. The prospect of twin sons loomed large. But at almost the same moment I felt tears come to my eyes. Here he was, my son, in the light at last. As he was handed to the pediatrician, I counted fingers and toes, watching the blue of his body give way to the pink of well-oxygenated blood. The pediatrician listened intently to his chest as the nurse gently suctioned his lungs. I nervously awaited his verdict. After a moment he smiled at me and said, "Perfect."

The nurse placed an ink pad against the soles of his feet and pressed them to a birth certificate. Two minutes old and already he was filthy. After being swaddled he was handed to me. We had not named him yet, waiting to learn what the next child would be. I sat on a stool beside Nancie, holding him up for her to see while both obstetricians began maneuvering the second baby into position. Should Nancie have required a cesarean, it would have become evident at this point. But I never gave it a thought, watching her smile through exhaustion and pain at our little boy.

The second baby dropped quickly into position. Our

doctor began calling out numbers—minus two, minus one, zero, plus one—as the head engaged the cervix and labor resumed. Sometime during that interval the anesthesiologist clipped a small oxygen tube under Nancie's nose to help her breathe. She was beginning to weaken, battered inside and out by two doctors and a pair of kids. Still she smiled at her little boy between contractions. He lay quietly in my arms, trying to adjust to this frightening new world of bright lights, piercing screams, and cold hands.

"Here comes the second one," the pediatrician whispered to me. I rose, still holding my newborn son, and stood beside the obstetrician. The head was already crowning, dark like the first. It will be another boy, I thought, trembling.

Then Nancie screamed, fluid burst from all around the baby, and the head slipped into the light. The obstetrician freed one shoulder, then the other. I glimpsed the genitals as he pulled the baby free and thought, It *is* another boy. In almost the same instant the doctor announced, "It's a girl." How could that be? I wondered. As he handed her to the pediatrician I realized that what I had taken to be a scrotum were extremely swollen labia, a common condition in newborn girls and proof, if one needs it, that all genitals develop from a common root. The nurse announced the time: 5:49.

Our daughter emerged in terrifying stillness, lying limp in the obstetrician's hands. He gave her to the pediatrician, who worked quickly to revive her. As the nurse suctioned her lungs, she began to squirm, then to cry. The doctor placed a small mask over her face, gave her a short burst of oxygen, and her skin reddened. Then the tears returned to my eyes. She was going to be all right. I laid my son on the warming table, took my daughter in my arms, and held her up for Nancie to admire.

"Have you chosen names?" the pediatrician asked.

Tears running down her cheeks, Nancie answered: David Alexander and Juliana Catherine. Five minutes later both babies were placed in isolettes and rolled out of the room to be weighed and measured.

Labor was not over yet. Nancie had still to expel both placentas. When finally she had done so, one of the nurses asked, "Should we send them to the lab to be tested for identical twins?"

"I don't think that will be necessary in this case," our doctor answered with a smile.

At 6:25 Nancie was wheeled into the recovery room. I was torn between caring for her and running down the hall to visit my newborn children. So for the next two hours I shuttled between recovery room and nursery, where the babies lay naked under warming lamps, heart-shaped temperature probes pasted to their chests. The overhead digital screen read 98.6. I stood between the two warming tables swelling with pride, wanting to shout to everyone who passed, "Come look at my kids!" Their weight had been recorded on cards attached to their isolettes: David, seven pounds, two and a half ounces; Juliana, six pounds, twelve ounces. Nancie had been carrying almost fourteen pounds of children!

Shortly after eight, Nancie was wheeled to her room across from the nursery. One by one I rolled our freshly swaddled babies to their mother, encountering, for the first time, the conflict that will be a part of my life hereafter: which one shall I take first? I chose David, the firstborn, returning a moment later for Juliana. While Nancie held one child, I held the other. We will never be empty-handed again.

At ten I finally tore myself away from Nancie and the babies. Elizabeth, flushed with exhaustion, shouted "Daddy!" and ran into my arms as I came to retrieve her from her grandparents. After teaching her the names of her new brother and sister I bundled her up, took her home, read her a story, and tucked her into bed. "See Mommy tomorrow?" she asked as I shut out the light. I promised she would, then stood outside her darkened room, listening as she sang herself to sleep.

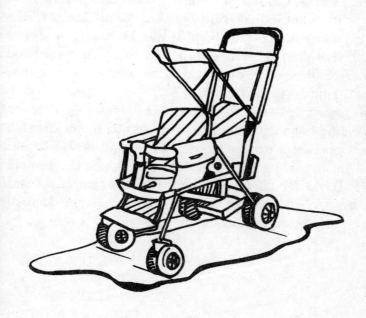

One final image: Before leaving the hospital, I wheeled the babies back to the nursery, placing their isolettes side by side. Just before David fell asleep he turned toward Juliana and closed his eyes. Moments later she too drifted off, facing her brother.

December 27

This morning, while Nancie nursed both babies, I spooned grapefruit slices into her mouth. "I feel like a juicer," she said with a wry smile. "Just shovel the fruit into my mouth and the juice runs out through my breasts." We needed a little humor just then. It was 11:30 and neither of us had showered, dressed, or eaten breakfast. As a seasoned mother of three once explained to us, you bathe one day, dress the next—if you're lucky.

The morning went as follows: David awoke at seven demanding to be fed; then Elizabeth sauntered in expecting milk, Cheerios, a dry diaper, and the Muppets. No sooner did I finish tending to her than Juliana joined the general melee. David demanded seconds, Elizabeth complained her milk was too cold, and while I changed Juliana the doorbell rang—Con Edison to read the meters—and so it went.

January 4

I calculated last night that in the thirty months since Elizabeth's birth, I have changed over six thousand diapers valued at roughly twelve hundred dollars. I will reach twice that number and more than twice the expense (thanks to inflation) by the time the twins are her age. Eighteen thousand diapers in five years! Fortunately, like all long journeys, this one will be accomplished one wet diaper at a time.

What, I shudder to think, is all that plastic, synthetic fiber, and adhesive tape doing to our environment? This house alone generates about eighteen dirty diapers per day. Imagine that nationwide. If all the disposable diapers soiled in one year were laid end to end . . . The mind boggles.

Did Tolstoy change diapers? I wonder. How about Dostoyevski? Balanchine, despite his many marriages, remained childless, so far as I know. While watching a TV documentary about him last night, I couldn't help comparing my life to his, wondering if it's possible to be a great artist and a devoted father as well. I suspect nature makes that choice for us. Clearly, I have been assigned to housekeeping. I was never much of a dancer anyway. But, oh, can my fingers pirouette around a Pampers.

February 4

The once-sacred orderliness of our lives continues to unravel. Our bed, which doubles as Nancie's office, is strewn with papers, catalogs, magazines, books, gift wrapping, and clothes. The stairs serve as a transit file, each step bearing something either on its way up or down: unwashed laundry at the top, clean laundry at the bottom; a new box of diapers two steps from the bottom, an empty box three steps from the top; three days of mail on three middle steps. The kitchen, which does time as a playroom, coat closet, and pantry, is crammed with boots, coats, gloves, cases of formula, overflowing garbage bags, and Elizabeth's toys. We need more space; it's definitely time to move.

Intending to reheat last night's lasagna, I infiltrated the kitchen this evening and gradually hacked my way to the refrigerator. But the pasta had disappeared. Like the rest of the house, our refrigerator defies description, a perfect example of Bachelor's Law—all foods, if left long enough at the back of a shelf, begin to resemble one another. Pickles look like mozzarella which looks like prunes which look like custard. I finally located the lasagna. It had been sitting in the oven since last night. The top layer resembled a desert waterhole in the dry season: stone hard, black, and cracked. I called in emergency burgers.

February 28

When we returned from our afternoon out with Elizabeth, Nancie asked if I had any cash to pay the baby-sitters. "Only a couple of twenties," I replied.

"That's fine," she answered. "I'll take both."

"For an afternoon of baby-sitting? Forty dollars!"

The price of childcare has gone the way of new cars, and

it doesn't help matters that we need two teenage girls to look after the twins. The underdeprived kids of our neighborhood earn three dollars an hour. Put two of them together for six hours and you begin to approach the stratospheric rates of trained baby nurses.

March 11

Nancie is becoming unhinged by the endless demands upon her. Most nights I return from work to find her prostrate on the bed, suffering back pain, headache, nausea, surrounded by crying babies and a willful Elizabeth.

"Another tough day?" I ask.

"Bonbons and soap operas," she replies. She's still in her nightgown, her morning cereal on the night table, uneaten.

"It's gonna get easier," I assure her.

"If I live that long. What do you do when you feel like quitting, but no one will accept your resignation?"

Just listening to her describe a typical morning would put anyone off their breakfast. Today she was determined to take a bath as soon as Elizabeth had been farmed out to my mother. But no sooner had she gotten one foot wet than Juli began crying. So she dried off, brought her into the bathroom, and succeeded this time in getting both feet wet before David started complaining. After settling him beside his sister she slipped beneath the warm waves. Then both children began to cry. So she jumped out, warmed bottles for them, and spent the next hour feeding, burping, and changing. Now I understand why I often find the tub filled with cold water. "I keep expecting to get back in," Nancie explained, "but never get the chance."

April 1

We've begun house hunting in earnest.

"I don't want you to just drive by this one," our realtor said this afternoon. "You've got to see the inside. It's you: light, airy, and tons of room. The family living there has twelve children."

Twelve children! How does one maintain one's sanity with a family that large? What car, short of a school bus, seats fourteen? Are that many children ever all asleep at the same time? ever all well? ever all quiet?

We entered the house through the kitchen, where the youthful-looking mother of this tiny nation stood surrounded by children ranging in age from the three-month-old she was changing on the kitchen table to the eighteen-year-old daughter cutting a younger brother's hair over the sink. The counters and floor were clogged with grocery bags being emptied and shelved by a team of elves. Every older child seemed to be shepherding a younger one while their ambidextrous mother not only changed her newborn and supervised the unpacking but managed to cook dinner as well.

"Are all these yours?" Nancie asked, careful not to step on any of the smaller ones crawling about the floor.

"Oh no," she said, pointing to one corner. "Those two aren't." They were the only dark-haired ones in a sea of blond heads.

I wanted to ask her how many quarts of milk she bought a week, how many pounds of spaghetti, how many loads of laundry she washed, but she was too busy to talk. We apologized for intruding and began our walk through the house, amazed by the woman's calm. I had thought all mothers of twelve were gray, squat, and perpetually weary. But despite giving birth a dozen times, she was still slim and upright.

In every room there were children: a son practicing the clarinet in the den, a daughter studying math in the living room, three kids jumping on upstairs beds, a teenage girl entertaining her boyfriend in the attic. The house was neat and tidy and surprisingly quiet considering the human density. It was also about half a million dollars more than we intended to spend.

On our way out we spoke briefly with the father, a tall, soft-spoken man in his mid-forties who was mowing the lawn while children trailed behind him, kicking up the freshly cut grass.

"Why are you moving?" I asked as he shifted the mower into idle.

"Five of the kids will be away at school next fall," he explained, leaning against the handle of the lawn mower. "We won't be needing such a big house for just the nine of us."

Just the nine of us!

MIXED MESSAGES

"I understand you have twins," the woman said over the phone. She had been given my name by her obstetrician, the same doctor who delivered Juli and David a year ago. "Do you mind if I ask you a few questions? I just learned I'm carrying twins myself."

I put down my book, settled into a nearby chair, and prepared to commiserate. "When are you due?"

"In five months," she said. "Should I be nervous?"

"Is this your first pregnancy?"

"No. We have a two-year-old daughter."

I stifled a laugh. "Do you plan to hire help?"

"Should I?" she asked.

I hardly knew where to begin. There was so much to tell, so much to conceal. After almost a year of raising twins, the first word that came to mind was *relentless*. Though normally susceptible to nostalgic longings, I still find the memory of those early months harrowing. Not that they lacked their own special pleasures, but I would not repeat them gladly, and certainly not without a small army of assistants.

Of course, one doesn't say such things to expectant parents. They will have time enough to discover the realities for themselves. Preparing for the arrival of children in duplicate is sufficiently unsettling without the added burden of excessive knowledge. So I hedged, mindful that there actually are parents of twins who insist that raising two is no more difficult than raising one, that their kids slept through the night from the first, that they never hired a day's help.

"We thought we could manage without assistance," I began, "but after a few days discovered we needed an extra pair of hands." (Actually, two extra pairs would not have gone to waste, I thought to myself.)

"I hate the idea of having a stranger in the house," the pregnant caller revealed.

"So did we, but you get used to it." (The alternative is insanity.)

"How did you go about finding someone?"

"Oh, there are dozens of agencies." (And none of them is worth a twenty-five-cent phone call.)

"Is it difficult choosing someone?"

"It helps to be a shrewd judge of character." (We're on housekeeper number nineteen.)

"How about sleep?" she asked, changing gears. "Do the twins wake each other up?"

"Occasionally, but not usually." (Except when they're running a fever and you're not feeling so well yourself and it's three in the morning.)

"How did your older child react?"

"She's very attached to them now, but in the beginning required some supervision." (She would have gladly dismembered them both.) "They mean well at that age, but don't yet fully understand the meaning of *gentle*." (Or of reasonable, quiet, or cooperative.)

"Was your wife able to nurse them?"

"She nursed for four months" (but the children required constant supplements).

"Would you recommend I join one of the local twins clubs?"

"They're great places to pick up advice and secondhand baby equipment" (and to have the daylights scared out of you by tactless veterans).

"Will I need anything special?"

"You'll probably want to double up on some things" (like your income).

"We're living in a two-bedroom apartment at the moment, so we thought we'd keep the babies in our room for the first few months."

"You could certainly do that" (if sleep is of absolutely no importance to you).

"I want to thank you for reassuring me," the woman said cheerfully. "I admit I was a little nervous when I first found out about the twins. But after speaking with you, it doesn't sound so overwhelming."

"It's not," I reassured her (especially if you can find someone to take your place for the first six months).

MOVING

LOST IN SPACE

To my eight-year-old eye it was a great white whale of a place, awesome, terrifying, beached far back from the road behind towering elms and dense, impenetrable brambles; all freshly painted brick and polished windows, the largest house I had ever seen.

"Is this it?" I murmured in amazement from the backseat of my father's 1959 Chevy, thinking with sudden terror: we aren't really going to live here, are we? Dad glanced over his shoulder, smiling with satisfaction as he turned into the long driveway. Almost overnight his fortunes had changed. Business had boomed, a fourth son had come along. The move he and my mother had been contemplating for three years was finally within reach. His chest expanded proudly. "This is it!" he replied.

The car slowly skirted one edge of the property, circled around before the mammoth front door, and came to rest. The sprawling lawn might easily have accommodated a football field, the driveway enough cars for a Fourth of July motorcade. The closer we came to the monolith, the more gargantuan it seemed, disappearing into the tops of ancient sycamores and oaks. This was not a house but an ocean liner run aground, complete with gangways, portholes, and funnels: two gleaming white chimneys topped with a stripe of black paint. All it lacked were lifeboats and circling sea gulls.

As the rest of the family left the car, I remained behind in startled disbelief, clinging to the familiar, head bent back, scanning the massive white facade for some sign of welcome, a friendly wink in the midst of so much imperial splendor. This new home bore as little resemblance to our domestic past as the Queen Mary to a rubber duck. Ladders had been thrown up on all sides, occupied by men in white coveralls. Here and there spots of red peeked through the white. Brushes passed over, the spots vanished. The task seemed herculean, a labor Alice might have encountered in Wonderland: so many bricks, so many ladders, so many buckets of white paint, so many scurrying workmen. It would not have surprised me if the house had suddenly risen a few feet, stretched its arms, and yawned, revealing an infinitude of spotted bricks beneath, prompting the sudden appearance of a hundred more painters equipped with a hundred additional ladders, paint cans, and brushes. Gulliver dwarfed the Lilliputians no more than this house did the cadre of workmen hanging from its gleaming white girdle. I was not accustomed to the scale.

I had spent my life in a small, red-brick colonial tightly wedged between neighboring houses on a street teeming with children, a street of gigantic families and diminutive homes, open doors and the perpetual keening of mothers calling in their young. Within that little house I had grown from infancy into consciousness, taking its measure as the natural and necessary limit of my security. It was the only house I had ever lived in, the only one I could imagine fleeing to and defending. Why should we move? We already had a home. In my eight years I could recall only one friend quitting the neighborhood, and that parting had seemed a kind of death. I could not envision his life elsewhere; he simply ceased to exist within the confines of the only universe that mattered: the block. To me there was no world "beyond Verona's walls." Outside its narrow streets chaos reigned in the sort of dark, unfathomable void the ancients pictured at the edges of their flat and finite universe. One might occasionally travel to such nether reaches—we did so periodically to visit relatives—but certainly one would never choose to live there.

Were we now to join the banished? For weeks my parents had talked of "the new house," lingering behind at the dinner table while my brothers and I, napkins trailing from our laps, hurried to join the general riot of unsupervised children out on the street. But I had ignored the hints—the wallpaper swatches, rug samples, paint chips, even the probing questions. Wouldn't I prefer to have a room of my own, a larger garden to play in, a modern new school to attend? A room of my own? What better place to sleep than the room I had inhabited all my life? A larger garden? Who needed one when the entire neighborhood served as our playground. And a new school? Fear and trembling lurked in the shadows of such a thought. What child would willingly walk into the dark and threatening thicket of a new school? My own elementary school had terrors enough, albeit familiar, manageable ones, eased by long consultation with trusted playmates. No thank you, I had no interest in moving.

We had, after all, just finished shifting my brothers around to accommodate the newest arrival, the fourth and final son. Wasn't that sufficient change? With the oldest now sleeping on a sofa bed in the den so that my younger brother could occupy the bed next to me, vacating the nursery for the baby and his nurse, I thought the transformation complete. My parents shared a room, why shouldn't we? Six of us in three bedrooms, a seventh downstairs. There wasn't a house on the street with fewer children. Our next-door neighbors numbered twelve, packed four to a room, clothes hanging from wall pegs and stored in baskets beneath bunk beds, shoes and sneakers tucked into sleeves hanging from the closet door, toothbrushes, dozens of them, sticking out of cups lining the bathroom windowsill. Theirs seemed an enviable congestion. Compared to them we weren't overcrowded, merely cozy.

But my parents had other ideas. As attached as they had become to the neighborhood, their first real home since fleeing Nazi Germany twenty years earlier, they wanted not merely beds but separate rooms for their children, not to mention greater privacy for themselves. A Castro convertible was a temporary measure at best. Growing boys required space, *Lebensraum*. The future prospect of sharing a house with four teenage sons no doubt played a considerable role in their deliberations. It was time to move on, move up. So they began devoting weekends and vacations to the search, walking through countless rooms, peering into cobwebbed attics and dank, musty basements, surveying gardens. What, ultimately, they found stood eight miles inland in an adjacent village where the streets were less congested, the houses larger and farther apart. We would not be moving immediately, my mother had assured me the day they broke the unsettling news, only after the painters and paperers had completed their work, after the roof was repaired, the kitchen remodeled, the floors scraped and carpeted. The house had long been neglected. It would take time to restore. In the interim, we would begin packing up the old, discarding all but the essential. She was intent on making a clean and uncluttered break with the past.

"But I don't want to move," I whined as the awful news sank in.

"Don't you want to have a room of your own?" she asked again, showing us a snapshot of the new house. I shrugged. For all my posturing, I was terrified of the dark, listening each night for the dread sounds of intrusion, the bed covers pulled up to my chin, wondering if my parents would hear my screams when the gypsies carried me off. I was convinced that bearded men in red bandannas and ebony-haired women in long, flowing skirts haunted the darkened streets. Like the Ishmaelites who had purchased Joseph from his jealous brothers and sold him into Egyptian bondage, they too trafficked in human flesh, stealing noise-lessly through unguarded doors and open windows to snatch sleeping children from their beds. That I had never seen one only intensified my dread. They were out there waiting just as certainly as the raccoons and skunks that rooted through the garbage while we slept.

And yet, despite my fears, I felt a certain security within those walls. For the house was small enough to be contained within my childhood imagination, circumscribed by my attentive ears. From any spot I could communicate with any other, sensing in an instant where safety lay, where terror lurked. Help was just a shout away, on the other side of the wall, across the hall, down the stairs. I knew the terrain and counted on familiarity to save me. No, I didn't want a room of my own. Who knew what dangers lurked within that omnivorous leviathan in the next town? For months it had lain empty, prey to all manner of night prowlers, vagabonds, hoboes—desperate, angry-eyed men who, at that very moment, were probably cooking their meager suppers in rusty tin cans over dirty candles somewhere in the nether regions of the limitless, unexplored attic. In such uncharted territory, anything was possible.

I tried my best to conceal such apprehensions. As the second of four sons, I understood the importance of appearances, of pretending to be fearless even in the face of overwhelming terrors. My older brother, ever on the watch for opportunities to declare me hopelessly effeminate, unfit company for someone racing boldly toward adolescence, was any father's ideal image of a son: tough, independent, courageous, determined to be a man before his time, craving nothing so much as a room of his own, a key to the front door, and a driver's license, though only ten. To him our impending move was heaven-sent, a chance to escape his childhood, wrap himself in glittering new robes, and burst forth the unchallenged hero of his own life.

I considered it pure catastrophe.

As I approached the front door of the new house, two moving men passed me carrying boxes, furniture, lamps, and paintings. Another two stood inside a huge moving van, wrestling our washing machine to the tailgate. I stopped to watch.

"You're just in time," the taller of the two said to me, jumping down from the van. "Come give me a hand with this, would you?" I smiled and shook my head, wondering how they had managed to get it on the truck.

"I'll tell you what," he continued. "I'll show you how to do this one and you can do the dryer." His partner wrapped a thick canvas strap around the machine and passed him both ends, which he crossed against his chest, arching back until the washer was pressed tightly to his spine. Then with a grunt he leaned forward, separating the washing machine

114

from the truck, hunched over like an aged pilgrim. He took two quick steps forward to steady himself, the machine rising above his back like some hideous growth, then began walking toward the house with a ponderous, elephantine gait, the muscles on his arms bulging through his dirty T-shirt. I followed him to the back stairs, keeping a respectful distance, awed by his strength. Step by careful step, he descended to the basement, first catching the machine in the narrow door, then crouching slowly until it cleared. On reaching the laundry room he knelt with the thumping hesitancy of a camel, then leaned back until the washer settled upon all four feet.

"Your turn," he said, wiping the sweat from his forehead as we returned to the truck.

"Guess you never had back trouble," Dad said, joining us in the driveway.

"Three fused vertebrae," the mover corrected, slapping his lower back.

"It's no wonder," Dad exclaimed.

"I didn't hurt it moving these things," he explained, taking a firm hold of the dryer. "Fell off a ladder painting my garage." A moment later the dryer was airborne.

When I finally entered the house I found it crowded with unopened boxes and sheet-enshrouded furniture. The movers had stretched runners of brown paper everywhere, converting the house into a sort of wilderness of footpaths. I called out for Mom, then followed her voice up the front stairs and down the hall to the nursery where she was busy emptying boxes of clothes into dressers. My little brother played in an empty carton while the baby slept nearby.

"Have you seen your room yet?" Mom asked. When I shook my head she walked me down the hall to a bedroom with a large bay window. A new carpet covered the floor; boxes bearing my name crowded one corner. My old dresser and desk were already in place. I stood by the window and looked out over the spacious garden. Below me lay the overgrown ruins of a maze, outlined in untrimmed boxwood, dominated by a crumbling fountain at the center of several converging paths. Behind it stood an open, unmowed field, and beyond that a decaying apple orchard choked with weeds and fallen branches. The rear boundary was lost in a dense forest of pines. For the first time since learning of the house, my interest was aroused. Here was something worth exploring, a primordial forest in our own backyard.

As the light began to fail the moving men slammed the van doors shut, presented Dad with papers to sign and a bill to pay, then climbed back into the cab and, with a belch of black smoke and the grinding of gears, backed slowly out of the driveway.

"We did it," Mom said with relief, standing by the front door watching as the loose-limbed trailer wandered onto the grass, clipping branches overhead. Rugs had been laid, furniture distributed, boxes unpacked. Much remained to be done, but the worst of it was over.

"It wasn't so terrible, was it?" Dad asked.

"It was awful," she corrected. "I'm never moving again."

That night we ate a hasty dinner of scrambled eggs and toast, then returned to our unpacking. The darker it grew the more apprehensive I became. How nice it would have been to climb back into the car and return to the old neighborhood, falling asleep amid the comforting murmur of my little brother's measured breathing and the sounds of children still playing out on the street, defying their mothers' threats. Through my new windows I heard only the scratch of crickets and the distant, muted bark of a dog.

I lay awake for what seemed like hours, listening with a fugitive's heightened sensitivity to the unfamiliar rattlings of the house. More than once I crept out of bed, cracked open the door, then sighed with relief hearing the muffled conversation of my parents downstairs. Just the sight of their distant light helped to quell my rising fears. In other rooms along the darkened hallway my three brothers slept. How did they do it so easily in this vast and unsettling place? I wished for their courage, or, lacking that, their company.

When I awoke the following morning, the sunlight was streaming through the bay window, bathing the wall beside my bed in orange and gold. I rolled over expecting to find my brother in the next bed, then remembering where I was, ran to the window. The garden was still in shadow, the grass glistening with dew. In the center of the boxwood maze stood two grazing rabbits. My fears had vanished with the coming of light. I ran into the hall and listened: silence. Still in my pajamas, I hurried down the stairs, stepped around cartons, and quietly let myself out. The sweet smell of freshly cut grass and the aroma of roses filled the air. I stood on the terrace surveying my new world. It seemed more paradise than purgatory now, filled with birdsong and bright light, a world worth exploring, one Alice herself might have envied.

As the sun began streaming through the trees I leapt down to the garden and approached the rabbits. They stopped chewing and lifted their heads, sensing danger. When they resumed their foraging I inched forward, the ankles of my pajamas soaked with dew. Finally, in a burst of

117

exhilaration, I lunged for them. They scattered in opposite directions, disappearing in the undergrowth. Alone, I turned back toward the house. It gleamed with celestial whiteness in the morning light, a ship of infinite possibility.

CRAMMING FOR COLLEGE

Ten years elapsed before I again changed addresses, this time without benefit of parents, eighteen-wheel tractor trailers, or moving men with fused spines. There were to be no complex packing schedules, no weeks of preparation, no wholesale family dislocation. I was going it alone, heading off to college, beginning the great odyssey of my life. And I was terrified. I felt none of the exhilaration that should have accompanied incipient independence, only grave misgivings and hollow, helpless fear. Was I ready to accept responsibility for my own future? I did not think so, not just then, not all at once. I would have preferred to ease into such an obligation, weaning myself gradually from the sureties of home step by tiny step instead of leaping blindly into the void. But the rules of conduct for my generation were unequivocal: middle-class high school graduates were expected to send themselves into voluntary exile for four years, jettisoning all or most of their past along the way. Sometime during that tumultuous period of self-discovery it was assumed we would launch ourselves into being, rocketing from the murky, rudderless anonymity of adolescence to the celestial incandescence of adult ambition. That I felt more gallows-bound than weightless on

118

the eve of my departure only proved the need for such enforced change. It was time to leave the nest, time to grow up.

How carefree, how effortless, how protected that earlier move seemed in retrospect. Back then I had only to follow orders. No difficult decisions had been thrust upon me: others had chosen when to move, what to take, and where I was to sleep. I simply stepped from one backdrop into another, finding my clothes and toys waiting for me in the same drawers in the same dresser. What fears I might have

had (and I had not forgotten them) seemed trivial in comparison to those now plaguing me.

For this time all the decisions were mine. I had chosen the city, the college, the field of study, even the dormitory. It was left to me to pack everything I owned or leave it all behind, to re-create as many of the comforts of home as my new accommodations would allow, easing the trauma of separation, or cast my lot with Spartan simplicity, trusting in a provident future. I chose some middle ground, carefully compiling a list of necessaries after long consultations with friends and relatives, then winnowing it down to the essential carful. Above all, I sought self-sufficiency.

Like my ancient ancestors, I planned to carry all my worldly possessions if not upon my back then upon my camel, or what passed for a camel among many eighteen-year-olds in America that year, a rusting two-door Camaro. The car contained a rear seat large enough to hold two small adults (knees firmly pressed against their chests) or three large cardboard boxes. The trunk, while shallow, reached well forward, and the passenger seat provided not only room on the cushion, but a deep foot well for large, leafy plants or bulky table lamps. Into these various cavities, one cool September morning, I wedged two bulging suitcases, a carton of records, a stereo receiver and turntable, two large speakers, a portable television, an electric typewriter, a duffel bag crammed with bedding, a desk lamp, a sheaf of well-thumbed piano music, an alarm clock, several pairs of shoes and sneakers, an overcoat, an umbrella, a plastic bag filled with toiletries, the latest *Life* magazine, and two brown paper bags containing enough tuna, canned fruit, Pop Tarts, instant cocoa, rye bread, Spam, dried figs, raisins, carrots, Ritz crackers, mustard,

120

and apples to last until my next visit home—probably within the month. Atop each bag my mother had placed an unopened tin of Danish butter cookies for the long, scholastic nights ahead. I lacked nothing for my journey into manhood but self-confidence.

Though my feelings were at odds with the custom, I had enough self-respect to follow the forms of my generation, having no wish to become an object of ridicule. There was already one such target in the neighborhood, an odd little man, prematurely bald, who, it was said, had never left home. Though somewhat better dressed than Harper Lee's Boo Radley and thoroughly unthreatening, he too seemed trapped in time, his growth unnaturally, pathetically arrested, a little boy dressed in men's clothing. As children we thought him mildly retarded, a conviction strengthened by his reclusive habits and slap-footed gait. He left the house only to walk his dog, always with eyes cast down, feet splayed, careful to avoid all contact with the neighbors. The only time we ever heard his voice was late at night when, through the darkness, he would call in the dog with a modulating falsetto whine—"Buddy, Buddy"—a poignantly appropriate name for what seemed to be his only friend. According to one story he had briefly attended college, but finding the pressures of emancipation overwhelming, had fled back home, never to leave again. What he did with his time no one knew, but it was universally assumed that he did nothing. His presence was a constant reminder to those of us frightened by freedom that without separation there could be no growth.

"Are you sure you've got everything?" Mom asked, standing by the kitchen door trying to conceal her tears as I circled the car. I was not anxious to be gone. The day was still young. I had packed more quickly than anticipated. So in the hope of delaying my destiny, I returned one last time to the house, making sure I hadn't forgotten anything, gathering my strength for the coming separation.

Already my room seemed alien. The bed had been stripped of its linen and pillow, the night table of its alarm clock, the desk of its lamp. I pushed in an empty dresser drawer, righted several fallen books, redistributed the few remaining clothes on the closet rod. Beneath them, piled in a dark corner, lay a dozen black-and-white theme booklets from grade school, ink-stained workbooks, dusty textbooks, certificates of achievement, report cards, cracked and curling class pictures, and my junior high school yearbook—ten years of scholastic memorabilia attesting to a lifetime of endeavor aimed at this very moment, my entry into college.

I peered one last time beneath the bed, then slowly surveyed my domain, self-consciously acting out the drama of my own departure. The soul of the place had already fled. It was just an empty room again, stripped of my imprint, looking very much as I remembered it the day we moved in. I walked to the window and looked out over the garden. In ten years much had changed: the boxwood maze and marble fountain had been replaced by two large rose beds divided by a sinuous flagstone path; a bolt of lightning had incinerated one of two towering spruces; age had claimed several apple trees, high winds a shallow-rooted willow, and time had transformed a skinny oak sapling into a formidable shadow. The fringes of the garden had not only remained wild, they had thickened. After the initial pruning a decade earlier, the perimeter had been allowed to pursue its own unruly inclinations, deepening the sense of calm and velvet isolation I so treasured. I would miss the garden most of all.

My father and two younger brothers had joined my mother beside the Camaro, the four of them peering in through the windows at the miracle of compression I had wrought.

"You still have room for a few pencils," Dad said, smiling. "How's the spare?"

"I couldn't get to it if I had to," I admitted.

"Call us as soon as you arrive," Mom said.

"Can I come?" my youngest brother asked, climbing in behind the wheel. Nothing would have pleased me more.

"We'll visit soon," Mom assured him. I opened the door and pulled him out of the car, then gave him a hug.

"You'll come up and stay with me some weekend," I promised, probably more comforted by the thought than he. Tossing my jacket into the back, I felt the sudden urge to be on the road, to leap over the dread moment of departure and hurry on alone. For weeks I had pictured this moment, afraid I might break down and reveal just how frightened I was of independence. I hardly knew the way to adulthood or even how to ask directions. In the presence of my little brothers, however, I assumed the bravura air of a young Jason, hugged them all, and assured my mother I would call as soon as I arrived. A moment later, arm waving, eyes fixed on the rearview mirror, I rolled out of the driveway, my dignity intact, my soul filled with mourning. I was witnessing the death of my childhood. Would I ever return? Would life ever be the same? I glanced up at the canopy of trees lining the quiet street, then lingered at the stop sign watching a mother and child playing in a nearby garden, my heart aching, craving nothing so much as home.

HOUSE HUNTING

It began barely twenty-four hours after Nancie discovered she was pregnant with Elizabeth. That first night she sat sketching nursery floor plans, researching Lamaze classes, compiling lists, charting our future, and finally announcing, "This house isn't going to be big enough for the three of us." Having focused my attention for so long on the problem of conception, I had given little thought to subsequent hurdles. For the next eight months, it seemed to me, no more material change was required in our domestic arrangements than the purchase of a maternity wardrobe. Thereafter, a small bedside cradle would serve along with a box of diapers and two or three diminutive outfits. How disorienting could those few acquisitions be? That the child would grow, would eventually need room to graze, did not yet occupy my thoughts. I was still reeling from the discovery of our long-sought-after expectancy, delighting in dreams of delivery. Of course our house would be large enough. How much space did a newborn require?

But Nancie was way ahead of me. She had spent the day on the telephone talking to seasoned mothers and grandmothers, requesting catalogs, pricing furniture. It was not too soon to begin our preparations, she insisted. We would need a crib and changing table, a dresser, new carpeting and wallpaper, a layette, teething toys, a stroller, baby bottles, warming dishes, bibs, spoons, pacifiers . . . The list was endless. Where would we put it all? she wondered.

"We have three bedrooms," I reminded her. "Two adults and two children should be able to live in this house comfortably." Besides, the question was academic. With the imminent loss of Nancie's income, I was in no position to assume the burden of a larger home.

"Then which room shall we make the nursery?" she asked pragmatically. One of them was actively employed as my office, the other as her studio. Giving up either would not only require considerable altruism on someone's part, but a complex reorganization of personal effects. The room I had transformed into a library shortly after our honeymoon was now crowded with more than two thousand books, a large desk, a computer, a cumbersome filing cabinet, and a reclining chair. The studio contained not only a drafting table and several dozen cartons of art supplies, but all manner of residual belongings, items on the periphery of Nancie's life with no place else to go.

Though I had never given voice to the assumption, whenever I envisioned a child among us (and I rarely thought of more than one during those lean, infertile years), I automatically placed it in Nancie's room. For while we referred to it as "the studio," it had never fully realized itself as such, drowning beneath its own contents. In another age Nancie might have been highly prized for her acquisitiveness, fashioning dresses from empty flour sacks, bast shoes from discarded hemp, children's toys from worn kitchen implements. To her the only waste was the failure to glimpse the living potential within inanimate objects. She recycled everything: used gift wrap, mail-order catalogs, chopstick sleeves. While ecologically commendable, such a trait had definite drawbacks in an era of high disposability.

"It's up to you," I declared, firmly believing that pregnant women should be indulged, whatever their idiosyncracies. I was not about to tamper with the delicate workings of a still-tenuous gestation by upsetting either Nancie or her studio. "I'll be happy to give up the study."

"What about all your books?" she asked.

"I'll just give them away," I declared, treating my most cherished possessions with calculated indifference.

"How could you? You love them."

"Something's got to go," I said pointedly.

"I can't let you give them up," Nancie decided with sudden generosity. "We'll just have to clear out the studio. But what do we do when the next child comes?"

"If the next one takes as long as this one, you'll be menopausal and I'll be in my dotage."

Nancie let the matter drop. She knew it was time to move, but also recognized that I was slow to accept change. "When you bet me," I often told her, "bet inertia." Sooner or later we would have to start looking for a new house. In the meantime she would make a few tentative inquiries, then gradually attach me to the process.

Shortly after Elizabeth was born, I found a familiar-looking telephone number taped to the refrigerator—our realtor's. Nancie was house hunting. Fine, I thought, let her look; no harm in that, so long as she understands I'm not moving. Our little house had never felt so complete, so like home. In less than nine months Nancie had transformed the studio from a hopelessly cluttered closet into an enchanting nursery. "How could you ever give this up?" I would whisper to her as family and friends admired not only our infant daughter but Nancie's decorating. She admitted it would not be easy.

126

Weeks passed and I heard nothing about moving. Nancie did not seem to begrudge the loss of her studio, too busy delighting in motherhood to think about other work. Life seemed perfect, and in my boundless naïveté I expected it to remain so. But then one evening over dinner Nancie mentioned she had just seen "a fabulous house: four bedrooms, a family room, a den, a small studio over the garage, and an eat-in kitchen." I stopped chewing, wondering just how serious this outburst was. "The only problem is location," she admitted. The house, it seemed, was situated at the intersection of two busy streets, and the garden was nothing much to speak of. Still, she insisted, it had a lot going for it, and, most important, it was reasonably priced.

"What's reasonable these days?" I asked, helping myself to salad, trying to remain calm. She quoted a figure normally associated not with real estate values, I thought, but the national debt.

I chuckled maliciously. "Who's got that kind of money? It's absurd."

"That's not a lot for a house these days," she insisted. "I've seen homes asking much more."

I choked on my salad. I had been vaguely aware of what inflation and the recent economic boom had done to local property values, but had not kept close track of prices. In the six years since we had purchased our house, Nancie informed me, it had appreciated 300 percent—or so our realtor insisted.

I searched hurriedly for a toehold among the rational, sensing the onset of a concerted campaign. "I don't want to start all over with mortgages and lawyers and closings. What could be more perfect than this?" I gazed down at

Elizabeth asleep in a basket beside the table. "I don't want to move. I like our life exactly as it is." I was beginning to get cranky.

Nancie dropped the subject, but not before mentioning the address and suggesting I drive by on the way to the station. Grudgingly, I promised to do so, if for no other reason than to assure myself that no house could compare favorably with the one we already owned.

And it didn't, at least not from the outside. But subtly, insidiously, a vague dissatisfaction began to take hold. Until that moment I had been indifferent to the lure of larger homes. I understood something of their demands and did not covet such responsibility, such crippling expense. But now gradually I found myself comparing and contrasting, newly conscious of enclosed porches, family rooms, eat-in kitchens. Our house really was small.

And then one day Nancie mentioned an address I had long admired, a house—to hear her describe it—capable of satisfying all my budding fantasies of improvement as well as her own. With little prodding she prevailed upon me to accompany her inside. In an instant I lost my innocence. Though we both agreed the place was not for us, I could not deny that for a moment, during the short drive from our house, I had felt a certain thrill at the prospect of change. The virus had taken hold. It was only a matter of time before I succumbed.

When, two years later, Nancie discovered she was again pregnant, the subject of moving was invoked with the greatest urgency. Who could deny the need? It was time to begin looking in earnest. In the meantime, however, I would vacate the study, moving my books to the living room. For eight years we had used it only to entertain. Why not take advantage of all that unused space?

It wasn't long before I had convinced myself that our little house might just possibly be made to accommodate the four of us for the long haul. Now was no time to move, not in the middle of a pregnancy with a demanding toddler sapping what little remained of Nancie's dwindling strength. Two small bedrooms, two small children, what could be simpler? Later, when the kids required more space, we could look for something larger or perhaps build an addition. In the meantime I intended to plunge my head into the sand.

But three months into the pregnancy we learned that Nancie was carrying twins. Suddenly, all bets were off. In a few months we were going to be the proud parents of three children under the age of three.

"How are we going to squeeze them all into our house?" Nancie wondered aloud. I had no idea.

"You'll love watching the thing take shape," our neighbor said, standing outside his recently enclosed porch. "The frame goes up almost overnight. You come home from work every afternoon to find it much farther along than you expected. You're sure they'll finish the job in a matter of weeks instead of months."

I smiled in anticipation of what was to come. I had heard many such tales in recent weeks. For the last month Nancie and I had been soliciting responses to the question, "Is it better to move or add on?" During walks through the village I questioned strangers whose houses had just been remodeled, hoping to find a reliable contractor. Thus far I had not succeeded. The experience of renovation, to hear them describe it, was somewhat akin to undergoing major surgery without benefit of anesthesia—an operation, moreover, lasting roughly twelve months.

"Did they finish on schedule?" I probed.

"Four months late," he revealed, "four frustrating, hair-pulling, teeth-clenching months late, on a job that was supposed to last only two. One moment everything was progressing beautifully, then out of the blue the contractor vanished. Every time I called his office I spoke to somebody else. Nobody knew anything. When I finally reached the foreman he gave me a long song and dance about back-ordered materials, men calling in sick, bad weather. 'Beginning of next week, for sure,' he promised. Baloney! They were working six other jobs at the same time. They all do. Once the frame's up they know you're stuck. It's too late to back out; the damage is done. All you can do is bitch. So while you're still admiring how quickly they work, they slip away to start their other jobs, playing round-robin, a few days with you, a few weeks away, servicing whoever screams the loudest. Gradually, the intervals between appearances lengthen. Weeks turn into months. You can't get them to finish." He paused again and smiled. "Still want to add on?"

"You tell me," I insisted.

"Maybe your experience will be better than ours," he admitted. "But it got so bad I finally threatened to sue the bastard. That had some impact but not much. The next day he returned, did a little more work, just enough to placate us, then disappeared again. Eventually, they wear you down. You grow weary of making so many phone calls, so many impotent threats. You begin spending more time at the office, find excuses to leave town frequently on business. When your wife calls, exploding with rage because the water has been off for three days, because the wind is howling through a hole the size of a refrigerator, because the garden has been chewed up by backhoes and frontloaders and the kids are tracking mud through the house, you blow up at her instead of at the contractor and insist she call the SOB herself. You're tired of taking the heat, of acting as intermediary. You never wanted the damn addition in the first place; you simply went along to please her. You threaten to sell the house, as is, holes and all, and move into a condo. Never mind that you went this route to avoid moving. You're just this side of homicidal, and virtually any victim will do—spouse, kids, contractors. Irrationality is the operative mode."

"What's the good news?" I asked.

"When the work is finally completed and you've had six months to live with all that new space, the extra closets, the late afternoon light, you begin to wonder how you ever did without it. The anger gradually dissipates, the contractor begins to seem less villain than hapless agent. Wasn't he doing his best, trying to please everyone? It wasn't his fault he was in such demand. And then one morning you find yourself writing a note or picking up the telephone to thank him for a job well done. Like childbirth, you've not only forgotten the pain, you're glad you went through with it."

"So I should add on?" I asked, not quite sure what conclusion to draw from his experience.

"I'd sooner spend a year in San Quentin," he declared.

I had put the denial phase behind me, committed finally to doing something significant about our living conditions. But resolve and solution did not necessarily go hand in hand. Indeed, the moment I determined to find a house, the market seemed to dry up. Suddenly demand exceeded supply. The prices made me laugh, then shudder. Not one of them seemed worth half what they were asking. But what choice did I have? Nancie was beginning to lose her mind, trapped indoors all winter with three noisy, exhausting kids and a husband out of touch with reality.

Every night over dinner the conversation oscillated between the twin evils: moving and adding on. Both terrified me, but with fluctuating intensity. One week I could more easily envision living among the dust, noise, and debris of major construction than I could packing up nine years of married life and transporting it to strange new quarters. But then a sudden change of heart would overwhelm me. Nothing endangered the bonds of marriage like remodeling, we had been warned. Better to move, whatever the physical demands, than risk emotional suicide through interior renovation.

Nancie was less ambivalent. She viewed construction as a last resort, something to be invoked only after every house in the village had been visited and found either wanting or grossly unaffordable. Whenever our realtor called she dropped whatever she was doing and rushed out to see the market's latest offerings. Weekends, I joined her, carping under my breath. Over the phone the listings always sounded so perfect. A master of architectural euphemism, our realtor knew just how to arouse our interest. Every house was "fabulous," every garden "lovely." The streets were always "quiet," the neighborhoods "charming," the neighbors themselves "delightful people." Each room came with its own commodious adjective: "spacious," "cheerful," "sunny." She dwelt on parquet floors, elaborate moldings, French doors, brass hardware. "You've got to see this one," she always implored, her voice full of excitement. "It's definitely you, and not unreasonably priced." There were never any shortcomings; her vocabulary lacked pejoratives. A small house was "cozy," "intimate," "captivating"; one that was hopelessly antiquated had "great potential." The worst ones, those with sagging floors, leaking bathrooms, and reeking kitchens, were "tired" or "in need of a little sprucing up," but always "exceptional values."

Six months of concerted house hunting passed without success. I didn't think we'd ever move, not only because the price of real estate was approaching the realm of long-distance telephone numbers, but because regardless of price, we hadn't seen anything we liked. I no longer dreamed of finding the perfect house; neither did I give much thought to adding on, but rather hoped to outlast the process, to survive the need for change and one day send Elizabeth and the twins off to college from the same doorstep they crawled over as infants. Still, Nancie persevered, hoping against hope each time our realtor called that her dream house lay waiting just around the corner.

When Nancie phoned a week after the twins' first birthday to say she was standing in the perfect kitchen, I knew by her tone we were about to cross the dread threshold from recreational house hunting to serious negotiation. There wasn't an ounce of reservation in her voice, not an iota of doubt. She sounded euphoric, almost delirious. Not only was the kitchen exactly what we needed, but so were the living room, dining room, bedrooms, and finished basement. "It's so light and airy," she bubbled, "and in immaculate condition." More important, she added, "it feels like home. There's nothing wrong with it, nothing. The elementary school is a block away. You can walk to the train. I LOVE IT!"

Always quick to sense the subtle fluctuations of my wife's feelings, I knew instantly this was not puppy love.

"What style is it?" I asked.

"Dutch colonial."

Our realtor said something in the background, coaching her.

"It's got a new roof, and they just relandscaped the front lawn and resurfaced the driveway. Everything's freshly painted. It looks wonderful."

"Put a bid on it," I suggested without considering the implications of my own words.

She caught her breath. "How can I? You haven't even seen it yet."

"I trust your judgment," I insisted. More important, I trusted the tone of her voice. I had not heard her sound so excited since Elizabeth and the twins were born. Here was a house that would help her forget that she spent her days cooped up with three small children.

"What should I offer?" she asked.

"What are they asking?"

She mentioned a figure. I paused. After three years of house hunting, I still wasn't used to the numbers. There were too many zeros. How did anyone ever afford to move? If we hadn't had a house of our own to sell, we would have been completely out of the running. I did some quick subtraction, the value of our tiny house from their medium-size house. The difference would determine how well I slept in the coming months. The remainder gave me pause.

"Offer ten percent less than they're asking," I suggested.

No sooner were the words out of my mouth than the bid was conveyed to the seller. Our realtor was standing in the sunroom on the other phone, speaking to the owner.

"Not enough," Nancie replied a moment later. "She says the house is fairly priced and will not accept less than asking, not yet anyway. It hasn't officially come on the market."

In our town, if the location is right and the price is within a certain range of the acceptably stratospheric, houses are bought before they ever go public. It works something like insider trading on Wall Street: word leaks out to a few chosen realtors, the quick jump in without a moment's hesitation, and the rest are left in the dust. Through a friend our realtor had managed to gain access the day before the open house. Ours was the first bid.

I counteroffered a few thousand higher. What was I doing? We didn't have that kind of money. I had no idea what my house was really worth beyond the inflated expectations engendered by wishful thinking.

Nancie shouted the offer to the sunroom, where it was relayed to the owner. This time there was some hesitation. "She won't accept our bid until you see the house," Nancie said a moment later. "Can you come home early?"

I could hardly refuse. All our efforts these last three years suddenly seemed focused upon this moment. What was the point of all those weekends spent traipsing through inadequate houses if we let the right one slip through our fingers? I left the office by the back door, caught an early train, and an hour later was standing alone with our realtor in the entrance foyer, prepared to be disappointed.

"Nancie is so excited," she reminded me, smiling broadly, watching my face for telltale emotional responses. I remained impassive, plugging all the leaks, determined not to be swayed by her real estate hyperbole. If I was going out on a financial limb to pay for this one, I would have to love it.

Nancie had been known to fall in love with a house for its French doors, its glass doorknobs, its dentil molding. She toured houses hoping to be delighted, overwhelmed. I, on the other hand, sought flaws, shortcomings, reasons to back out. But on this occasion, after an hour's careful inspection, I found none. There was nothing I didn't like about it, and not for want of trying. I rapped my knuckles against walls—solid; peeked into basement corners—dry; probed the attic—spacious; examined the electrical system—new. The noose tightened.

"So what will they accept?" I asked, the two of us standing in the kitchen, watching the sun drop behind the distant cupola of the elementary school. Nancie had been right, it did feel like home, only better.

"Asking price," she said with a shrug of her shoulders.

"Nothing less?"

"Sorry."

"So offer."

"You won't regret it," she said, rushing to dial the phone.

In that moment I expected trumpets, music, lights, the fanfare of astronomical expenditure. If I were selling a house for that much money and found a buyer before officially putting it on the market, I certainly would have let out a howl of satisfaction and slapped the nearest back in rapturous disbelief. But when our realtor finally reached the owner and conveyed the news, the woman received it with a poker player's insouciance, saying only, "I accept." That was it. No words of gratitude, no praise for my good taste, no assurances that I had made the right decision and would be deliriously happy there, just simply, "I accept."

Ten minutes later my burgeoning family drove up. When I ran out to meet them Nancie asked, "So, what do you think?"

"It's sold," I replied, straight-faced.

"What do you mean 'sold'?" she cried in astonishment. "How could it be? To whom?"

"To you," I said with a hug. "Welcome home."

BESET BY BEARS

I took a census the other morning. Six months after moving I noticed the corners of our new house beginning to narrow. Having just gone into hock to the tune of half the gross national product of Burundi to escape that feeling of confinement, I called the family together and took an informal head count. These are my findings as jotted down on the back of last month's Con Ed bill: one father, one mother, one older sister (age four), one set of fraternal twins (age two), one life-size Raggedy Ann, two giant pandas, four Snoopies, five Barbies (with extensive wardrobes), seven multicolored clowns, eight plastic babies with hinged eyelids, nine kittens (mostly gray), eleven plush bunnies (mostly white), fifteen basic brown dogs, and ninety-seven teddy bears (assorted sizes). Total population: one hundred and sixty-four.

When I confronted Nancie with these figures she simply smiled. Teddy bears, she informed me, tend to congregate in homes with small children, as do baby-food jars, rattles, and disposable diapers. I glared at her over the top of my glasses. Did she mean to deny responsibility for this infestation, to declare in all sincerity that ninety-seven plush teddy bears (mostly brown) had wandered into our house without her assistance? Yes, she said with a smile, that's basically what had happened. To be sure she had made a few early purchases before the children were born, driven by an expectant mother's hormonal needs, but lately she'd hardly bought one.

"What about the huge cardboard box I saw you unpack yesterday?" I probed with infinite skepticism.

"Your mother sent it for the twins' birthday."

"And the shopping bag you snuck in through the kitchen the day before?"

"A surprise for Elizabeth from my sister." Then before I could question her further, she took the offensive.

"What's wrong with having a few teddy bears around the house?"

"Six or seven is a few—I could live with that—ninety-seven is an epidemic, a plague. What do we need so many for?"

"You might as well ask why we need so many children," she replied calmly.

I studied her face in genuine dismay. "How can you equate stuffed animals with flesh-and-blood children?"

"Because each one is different," she said, picking two up from beside the couch. "How can you resist them?" Her voice assumed the high-pitched, treacle-rich tone usually reserved for newborns and puppies. "Aren't these two of the sweetest faces you've ever seen?"

Having seen ninety-five others with roughly the same features, I took her by the hand and walked down to the playroom, where the majority of her menagerie congregated. Arrayed on four long shelves, they sat shoulder to shoulder wearing the same slightly bemused expression: teddy bears, basic, brown teddy bears, virtually identical. Describing a wide arc with my arm, I declared: "These all look alike to me."

"Forgive him," Nancie whispered to her charges. "He doesn't mean it."

"I most certainly do," I declared.

Then she did an astonishing thing. She named every one of the thirty bears on the top shelf: "Winston, Clarence, Annabelle, Oscar, Maxwell, Shakespeare, Oliver, Julius, Miranda, Kingston . . ." All the way to the end of the row. She then began on the second row and would have continued, I suspect, through all four shelves had I not stopped her and pointed to a single bear she had already named and asked, "Who is this?"

"Clarissa," she said without hesitation.

"And this one?" I asked, pointing to another out of sequence.

"Seymour."

I turned her back to the shelves, mixed up the bears, and then asked her to name them again. She replied instantly and correctly with a mother's unerring eye, then returned them to their proper places. I was clearly out of my depth.

And then, as if to confirm my ursine isolation, Elizabeth wandered down to the playroom in search of Teddy, *the* Teddy, her boon companion and bed buddy, the albino bear that had eased her into sleep every night since we brought her home from the hospital four years ago.

"Why don't you suggest she take one of these instead?" Nancie declared in jest. Even I understood that offering Elizabeth another bear in Ted's stead would have been akin to suggesting a mother return home from the playground with the nearest available child.

"Well then, you do understand," she announced, trying to force me to concede ground. "No one can replace Teddy."

"Alright, maybe they aren't all the same, but why do we need ninety-seven of them?"

"I might ask you the same of your library," Nancie averred, walking me up to my study and pointing to a row of identically bound volumes. "Elizabeth once asked me why you had so many of the same book," she recalled. "I tried to explain that they weren't the same, that they only looked alike until you got to know them."

"They only look alike to her because she can't read their spines," I retorted.

"My point precisely," she said, smiling. "The bears look alike to you because you can't read their expressions, because you don't appreciate how different their personalities are." She gathered up three waiting for her just outside the study and pointed out significant differences in fur, face, and feet.

"But they don't contain anything of substance, nothing but hypoallergenic polypropylene fibers; you can't read them, they're not alive, they just sit there taking up valuable space, gathering dust—hemming me in!"

" 'There are none so blind . . . ,' " she began.

Sensing impending defeat, I decided to alter my tone from aggressive inquiry to obsequious supplication. "Will you at least do what you can to stabilize the population? Ninety-seven is enough, isn't it?"

"It's out of my control," she insisted.

I groaned. We were back to square one. "But we just moved and already we're running out of room. What will we do if another child comes along?"

"I guess we'll just have to put it back in its carton and return it," she said, smoothing the ruffled fur of one of her charges. "They all look alike anyway."

MY GENERATION

FACING THE FIREBALL

My father did not expect his children to reach adulthood, not in the late 1950s when the threat of nuclear war seemed so imminent. I was only just emerging from the cocoon-like oblivion of early childhood as the Soviet Union began its atmospheric testing of hydrogen warheads, sending millions of Americans scrambling for cover. Every morning the newspapers carried new revelations about the extent of Russia's massive nuclear capabilities, pessimistic reevaluations of our eclipsed superiority, charts comparing the latest megaton detonation to the tiny kiloton device that incinerated a hundred thousand Japanese in Hiroshima. Our milk, we learned, contained traces of strontium 90, the radioactive fallout carried from Pacific and Siberian testing grounds on apocalyptic winds. Public buildings began setting up civil-defense shelters, stocking their basements with water, wafers, and Geiger counters, while school-children were instructed, in the event of nuclear attack, to take refuge beneath their desks, cover their heads, and look away from the fireball. Khrushchev shouted, "We will bury you"; we responded, "Better dead than red"; the *Bulletin of the Atomic Scientists* set its clock hands a few minutes closer to the midnight of human extinction; and my father sat down to dinner one night and told his two young sons that the world would probably not last another ten years.

I was too young to argue the point. At six years old I

hardly knew what to make of all the hysteria I sensed on the periphery of our quiet, suburban life. That something had changed I vaguely understood, but I successfully ignored the unsettling feeling aroused by the late-night conversations I heard across the hall until my father finally identified the source of his preoccupation. Then all at once I was seized by the terror that had been lurking in the shadows of my mind. My parents no longer controlled my destiny; other, hostile forces did. An atomic sword dangled above our heads, threatening us with extinction, and no one, not even my omnipotent parents, could remove it from our midst.

My older brother, marshaling all the persuasive powers of an eight-year-old, tried to convince my father that he was wrong, that we would survive just as parents and children had always survived. Why should our generation be singled out for annihilation? God would not let it happen.

Why then, my father responded, his voice heavy with pessimism, had his own generation suffered near obliteration during the Holocaust? Why had a million Jewish children been incinerated in the ovens? Those who had insisted it could not happen were the first to die.

Tears welled up in my eyes. Were we all going to perish? My brother resisted the conclusion. If reason could not persuade, then passion would have to suffice. We were not going to die, he declared. It wasn't fair.

Life wasn't fair, my father insisted. Most of the time it was exceedingly cruel. At that my brother began to sob his terror and frustration, blaming my father for the treachery he had just unearthed. If he would only take back his words, we both fervently believed, our confidence would be restored, our lives secured. He had the power to remake the

146

universe, even to declare us immortal if he chose; we would have believed him. But he could not. His past would not permit him to do so. My father had compelling reasons for steeling us to our fate. He had survived a world war that taught him one inexorable lesson: blind optimism kills. Those of his kinsmen who had shrugged off the danger and remained behind in Germany, believing the thread would hold, that the sword would never fall, perished in the carnage that followed. So if my father taught his children anything, he was determined to leave us with open eyes and a shuddering appreciation of the real and present danger. Better to face the truth squarely than walk blindly to the ovens.

For months afterward I suffered nightmares of destruction. Every passing plane terrified me. Fire Klaxons sent me scrambling to the radio for news of an atomic attack. And school air-raid drills, once a welcome break from routine, left me cowering under my desk, head covered, praying for the all clear with a fervor that only the fear of death can summon.

After that night we never discussed the subject again, at least not in such portentous terms, and gradually my dread of a fiery death ebbed until it seemed just another baseless terror of childhood. Even when, four years later, during the Cuban Missile Crisis, nuclear war seemed less a speculation than a probability, we did not speak of annihilation but of methods of survival, discussing where to build a bomb shelter. Somehow, within a few short years, we had grown accustomed to living with nuclear weapons and expected to survive if for no other reason than that we had done so until then.

We were the first generation in history to grow up in the

shadow of global annihilation, the first with the potential to be the last. *Après moi le deluge* was not a conceit but a terrifying possibility. And because we were the first, our parents and teachers were ill equipped to sensitize us to our condition. Indeed, with the exception of my father that one bleak night, no one ever spoke of our vulnerability. They ignored the abyss, neither preparing us to build bridges across it nor to face down into the darkness and sound its depths. They merely hinted at its presence and left us to deal with it as we chose. And we chose, for two decades, to disregard it.

Repressing our fears in a frenzy of good works, we integrated schools and buses in Alabama and Mississippi, inoculated children in Ethiopia, taught in Harlem, and finally decried America's involvement in Vietnam. In retrospect the passion that drove us into the streets during that war seems as much an expression of our frustration, of our inability to alter the basic terms of our delicate existence, as it was a reaction to the carnage in Southeast Asia. When we spoke of peace and emblazoned its symbol across our lives we were concerned with more than a regional conflict, we were thinking globally. Yet during the 1960s we rarely talked of the bomb.

Curiously, during those same years American taxpayers supported the expenditure of billions of dollars to land a man on the moon, a goal that seemed to serve no other purpose than to provide a psychic escape valve, a fanciful, unspoken option in the event of thermonuclear war. Our world might be doomed to self-destruct but still we might survive, abandoning it in the eleventh hour as bombs rained down upon those who remained behind. We needed that option, if only in fantasy, to keep the terror at bay, knowing, despite our seeming indifference to the missiles in our midst, that man had never invented a weapon he had not used. If history demanded that our world perish then our only future lay in the gleaming white rockets that hurled Americans into space.

No one had foreseen that by the mid-seventies the very resources that fueled our national dream would fail us. Prices rose, supplies fell, and we awoke as if from a fool's paradise, wondering how we could have squandered so much for so long upon so few. Then too the war in Southeast Asia was winding down; we needed another diversion, Armageddon still threatened if we admitted it. So to occupy our thoughts we worried instead about the price of coffee and where to find enough gasoline to fill our tanks. Instead of looking for ways to ensure our perpetuation we labored to produce automobiles capable of transforming a gallon of gas into thirty miles of errands. Where we intended to go didn't much matter, there was no escape. But we needed to feel that we were the chauffeurs of our own fate, that come what may, at least we could pilot ourselves to oblivion, keeping the fireball in our rearview mirrors. It was easier to worry about inflation, about the failure of the steel industry, about the scarcity of heating oil than it was to consider what one false move in our nuclear china shop would mean. Blindness had worked well for twenty years. There was no reason to believe it wouldn't continue to preserve us.

But then the 1980s dawned, a new president spoke of rearming America, and suddenly we reawoke to the fragility of our world. In a spasm of conscience we picketed weapons manufacturers, military bases, and political leaders. Chain-link fences were scaled; ominous white trains, suspected carriers of nuclear warheads, were blocked; in New York a million people marched in support of peace; and petitions were signed from one end of the Western world to the other, calling on America and the Soviet Union to freeze the production of nuclear weapons. As if the subject had only just been discovered, new books appeared in staggering numbers, filling a seemingly insatiable appetite for information about the danger so long ignored. Where had we been for twenty years that frank discussion about the effect of an atomic blast over Kansas City gripped us with such horrifying fascination? What had we thought would happen underneath those mushroom clouds that had long since become a symbol of our age? We had seen the newsreels from Japan in the wake of *Enola Gay*, we knew what happened to cities and their occupants when exposed to radioactive fallout. Why did it suddenly seem so unexpectedly threatening?

Then the skeptics entered the arena, insisting there was nothing we could do to eliminate the menace. It was too late. We should have thought of that in 1943. Nuclear weapons were an unpleasant fact of life, but a fact nonetheless. The only means of protecting ourselves was by preserving the status quo, the threat of mutual assured destruction. Freezes were unverifiable, the enemy was un-reliable, and while we tarried over misguided disarmament proposals, precious time was being lost in the battle to domi-nate space with new weaponry.

In the midst of this rediscovery of our precariousness, my three children were born. Contrary to my father's pessi-mistic predictions of twenty-five years ago, his children had not only survived the 1970s, they had lived to see parent-hood. Yet still his words linger, not in mockery of him, but as a chastening reminder that we are no more secure today than we were that night in the late 1950s when he saw only blackness and death. Nothing has changed. Indeed, if every bomb is a sword and every passing year wears upon the thread suspending it above our heads, then we are in far greater peril today than we were during my childhood.

Will I tell this to my children? Will I, for their own sake, try to impress upon them the fragility of this world, of all life, as my father had done? I don't think so. Not only because of the pain it will cause them, but because I cannot, in good conscience, charge them with the responsibility of solving a problem I was not even willing to confront. My generation, the most combative and committed to change in modern history, accomplished nothing to secure its own future. How then can I expect my children to succeed?

I will not present them with a future that bodes only annihilation because, in truth, I do not believe, despite the enormous hazards that face us, that we will end in a flash of blinding light. The voice of the six-year-old clinging to life under the benevolent eye of God has not abandoned me. I fully expect my children to see adulthood and in time to sit beside their own children and explain the harsh realities of life honestly but with hope. My father too eventually found his optimism. Somehow we all expect to survive.

WET HAIR

On a bitter cold morning last week I watched the steam rise from the hair of a young woman waiting for the 7:56 express to Grand Central, her long, wet strands crystallizing in the wind. She stood beside another wet-haired woman and an equally damp-headed young man. All three of them wore miniature headphones. Their breath condensed in small clouds between them as they talked.

Apparently impervious to the deep frost, the young man waited with his coat open, collar unbuttoned, tie askew. Neither he nor the women wore hats. Hadn't their mothers taught them not to venture out in the dead of winter with a wet head? Apparently not. Or perhaps newly achieved independence and the inability to budget enough time for the hair dryer had overcome the injunction. Fortunately, they had the resilience of youth on their side. Fresh out of college, they and half a dozen other young commuters stood glistening on the platform each morning, taking their place in the work force with an energy that distinguished them from the rest of us waiting for the train.

I enjoyed watching them, reminded of my own entrance into that world a decade ago. There were fewer women then, the platform crowded with drab, inanimate clusters of gray overcoats and hats that rode to the city in concentrated silence. This new generation of women had added not only color but vitality to our morning vigil. Wearing sneakers and white athletic socks over stockings, they seemed possessed of a Mercury-like urgency that bubbled up in their conversations and burst forth the moment the train arrived in Grand Central. Unhampered by the high heels and tight skirts of an earlier era, they bolted from their seats and up the stairs before the rest of us had folded our newspapers.

The young men added their own stamp as well, wearing conservative three-piece suits but with shoes more often tan, blue, or light gray than the traditional brown or black of their fathers. In addition to the *Wall Street Journal* they carried copies of *Rolling Stone* magazine, and a few sported

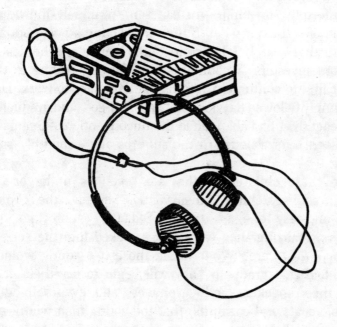

a single diamond earring, a subtle reminder that this new generation was no carbon copy of the old.

I have not been riding the rails long enough to qualify as a veteran. My ten years on the Harlem line seem paltry beside the four decades of my neighbor. But in the presence of these younger commuters I have begun to feel shouldered out of youth, relegated to that older generation of brain-dead bureaucrats we used to mock during the self-righteous sixties. How did it happen? I sometimes wonder. How did I end up within the ranks of those we ridiculed for marching on and off the train with automatonlike regularity, rain or shine, summer and winter, until stopped by heart attack or retirement?

I had sworn in college never to succumb to the comforts of conformity, to pursue instead some uniquely individual avenue of self-expression. But after devoting a postgraduate year to that search I had reluctantly joined the hordes of itinerant investors, accountants, and lawyers, riding to the city at first to continue my education and later to work. Day had simply followed day, seasons had changed, and gradually, even eagerly, I had abandoned the unconventional dreams of adolescence for a house in the suburbs and a monthly paycheck.

Had these children of the late seventies undergone a similar soul-searching transformation, or had the choice been an easy one for them? Did they appreciate the dangers, realizing they were being sucked into the vortex, or didn't they care? What would those two young women say if told that gradually they will begin to dry their hair, shed their sneakers and earphones, and eventually don sensible coats and earmuffs; that the young men will begin to lose their hair, carry pictures of their children, and wear brown wing tips and odd-looking hats with earflaps?

They would probably respond, "We know." They had not entered college seeking to reform society, but to acquire the tools necessary to do battle in the business world. They boarded the train with both eyes open, aware of the sacrifices such a life required. Still, the sight of them each morning evoked a twinge of melancholy.

Last week, as I sat beside one of the young women, the volume in her earphones so loud I could hear the music across the vacant seat separating us, an old high school acquaintance of hers slipped into the empty place, his wet hair glistening. Smiling, she slid the headset down around her neck and launched into a carefully choreographed conversation. Each question was phrased to elicit the identical question in return, queries about college, degrees, apartments, jobs, and rediscovered friends from high school. Eager to impress each other with how much they had accomplished in the two years since graduation, they exchanged titles, detailed descriptions of their responsibilities, and dropped the names of famous people they or their associates knew.

I remembered those conversations from my own past. How important it had seemed after college to represent myself as a breadwinner, a responsible, productive member of society. I never regretted the decision; but winter mornings when the switches froze and we stood for an hour in the bitter cold, I wondered what it would be like after forty years to look back over a life spent shuttling between a bed in the suburbs and a desk in the city. Did the old men seated beside me regret the roads not taken, or had they long since made their peace with a life of unalterable routine? No doubt they were content to let others scale mountains. But I was still mindful of the sacrifice, believing in darker moments that all of us on that train were wasting something precious in our pursuit of stability.

As we neared Grand Central the young man began to dominate the conversation. Every few sentences his companion, her hair nearly dry, responded, "Really, that's great," as he detailed his triumphs on Wall Street. Her tone was genuine but reflexive, as if she had begun to glimpse the emptiness of such achievements. Get off this treadmill before it's too late, I wanted to tell her. Don't take the bait. Go pursue those other dreams. If you fail, you can always come back. We'll still be here waiting patiently for the 7:56.

DREAD VISIT

I was shocked by how gaunt he looked, dozing beneath a thin hospital blanket, surrounded by flowers, get-well balloons, and books on spiritual healing. He lay propped up by pillows, his right arm behind his head, his left hooked to an intravenous line, a magazine open on his chest. Six months ago we had euphemistically referred to him as robust; he knew how to get full value from a meal. But since the onset of illness he had lost his appetite, developing within a matter of weeks the wasted, haggard appearance of someone enduring great suffering. His head and hands seemed too large for his sunken chest; his cheeks, once round, now clung tightly to his jaw. The very vitality he used to exude had abandoned him. Even his smile had changed. While still welcoming, it betrayed a deep, consuming preoccupation. So did his eyes. But for a moment, as I pulled a chair beside him and patted his forearm, they flickered with the old pleasure of receiving company.

For days I had dreaded the visit. What would I say to him? How could I assume a tone of hopeful encouragement without sounding forced, artificial, contrived? Would he want to talk about his condition? Would I do him harm by referring to it? By ignoring it? When a man breaks a leg one makes jokes, accuses him of clumsiness, anticipates a speedy recuperation. The initial shock of disability rapidly yields to the conviction of recovery.

But when the diagnosis is cancer, both the landscape of mortality and the language of commiseration change. No one makes jokes at the patient's expense. Life, once endlessly expansive, becomes suddenly constrained by the pitiless, narrowing walls of a too-certain finality. What room remains for hope? How does one talk about the future when the future seems so brutally foreclosed? Doesn't the very presence of the healthful serve as a cruel reminder of the capriciousness of nature, of the widening gulf between illness and well-being? Unsure of my role in this unfolding tragedy, I dreaded causing yet more pain through ignorance and thoughtlessness.

The news of my friend's cancer terrified me. Why him? Why not me? We were the same age, lived in adjacent communities, pursued similar lives of sedentary labors punctuated by vigorous exercise. Nothing in his profile typed him a potential casualty. Nothing protected me from suffering a similar fate.

In illness as in crime, we tend to blame the victim, finding cause in petty frailties and bad habits. When the heavy smoker develops lung cancer we sigh with sympathetic superiority: he should have known better. While we attribute our own misfortunes to a malicious fate, we pin the fate of others on their shortcomings, scrambling for distance, for a rationale to interpose between ourselves and the motiveless malignity of nature. We seek refuge beneath the sheltering wing of genetics, grateful for the security that comes from knowing that certain afflictions are simply in the blood—so long as they are not in our blood— that while nature may indeed be capricious, it exempts certain parties from whim. Even the godless believe in a form of divine justice, convinced they can avoid such a fate through right thinking, right living, right eating.

But I found little security in such thoughts. There was nothing in my friend's history, no evident genetic disposition, no ancestral record that might explain why a thirty-six-year-old man would suddenly develop a malignant tumor. Health had suddenly given way to disease and no one could explain why.

During the first strained minutes of my visit I inched toward this new reality, cautiously avoiding mention of his cancer, trying to discover the territory he now occupied and its terms, wondering how he had taken the news, and how, if our roles were reversed, I would have. Initially, he responded with uncharacteristic stiffness, his mind operating in another, hidden realm. Then, suddenly, he pronounced the dread word himself. The window open, I approached cautiously and peered through. "When did you first find out?" I asked.

Slowly and with increasing candor he spoke of his ordeal:

the checkup, the discovery of a tumor, the emergency hospitalization and biopsy, and then the verdict. "The first three days here I was all smiles and good cheer," he said. "Somehow I managed not to think about it as long as we were waiting for the biopsy results. Then they told me the bad news and my mind started careening out of control." In the first blinding instant of discovery he told himself he was dying, that in six months he would be gone. He considered taking his own life rather than drifting hopelessly, helplessly toward oblivion. Better to end quickly and vigorously than in feebleness. But in time his religious conscience stirred; such thoughts were sinful. Alone in his hospital bed he paddled around in darkness, searching for some safe harbor, unable to sleep, wondering what was to become of him.

"Around midnight I asked the nurse for a sleeping pill," he told me. "When she returned I realized how desperately I needed to hold someone's hand, to restore contact with life. I had never seen her before, but when I reached out, she took my hand and asked what was wrong. I just broke down and cried. She remained by my side until I drifted off to sleep. I haven't seen her since."

How did he feel now? I wondered, two weeks after receiving the verdict. What did his mind do with the knowledge of mortality? Could he continue to hope?

Blessedly, most cancer patients do. Instead of focusing on the distant future, they look inward, their horizons contract: they think in terms of days and weeks, concentrating on immediate challenges, small setbacks and minor gains. For my friend the imminent removal of his intravenous line filled him with great hope, signaling, if only temporarily, a return to normalcy. He was looking forward to spending a few days at home before transferring to another hospital.

The prospect of such freedom, of familiar surroundings, peace, and privacy shielded him from thoughts of what would follow: chemotherapy, surgery, radiation. At the moment he was thankful to be over the pain of his biopsy. He would deal with the future one day at a time.

As he spoke my friend reached out and took my hand. "You'll beat this," I said. At that moment I truly believed he would, no more willing to accept defeat than he was.

"I'm certainly going to try," he insisted, wincing as he shifted in bed. He had risen up out of the valley of the shadow of death and was prepared to do whatever life required. "I've got the rest of eternity to be dead," he declared with brutal forthrightness. "As long as I've got the strength, I'm going to fight."

I leaned over and kissed his hand, doubtful that, in his place, I would have such courage.

SUNDAY MORNING SOFTBALL

They were an odd assortment of men, ranging in age from mid-twenties to mid-fifties, from lean and fit to hopelessly out of shape, dressed in everything from grease-stained madras shorts and black dress shoes to regulation baseball knickers and cleats.

I had stumbled upon their Sunday softball game shortly after moving to the neighborhood, pulling off the road one windy morning in early spring, my car full of groceries, intending to watch only an inning or two. But within minutes I had crept closer to the bench, suddenly hoping, like every boy who ever dreamed of glory, that someone would toss me a glove and send me out into the field. Nothing arouses the unresolved conflicts of childhood as keenly as baseball.

I suffered no delusions of athletic prowess; baseball has never been my game. Still, I have always found the camaraderie of the sport alluring. From a distance the men who come together on summer evenings and Sunday mornings seem a world unto themselves—relaxed, intimate, content. In high spirits, they mock each other, share their gloves, congratulate skillful plays, and delight in being temporarily free of all other responsibilities. Say what you will about the banality of the game, its deadening pace and lack of action, those who play seem to revel in the suspension of time, forgetting for a few hours that they run multinational corporations, have just been fired, are headed for divorce, or require root canal.

Standing outside the low stone wall that edged the field, I looked for someone among the dozen players who might welcome me. I could think of no quicker entrée into the community, no better way of gaining acceptance—short of suffering through hours of tortured cocktail conversation—than joining that game. So I ignored my melting ice cream and inched over to the bench, trying to appear conspicuously interested without groveling.

I hadn't played softball in years, not since high school, yet by some genetic predisposition I had dutifully carried my glove along the tortuous path to adulthood, packing it in my camp trunk, squeezing it into a corner of my college duffel, and stowing it in the front closet of every apartment I had rented since graduation. When Nancie and I moved to the neighborhood the glove moved with us, taking its customary place on the top shelf of the hall closet, ready to be pressed into service.

That it would fit I never doubted; indeed, in all likelihood it would still be too big. My father had bought that glove for my tenth birthday, choosing one, as he put it, with ample room for growth. My ten-year-old hand reached barely halfway into the smooth, aromatic fingers then, but I loved it all the more for its being an adult glove and looked forward to one day filling it out. During that season of my grand infatuation with the game, I wore the new mitt around the house, slamming my fist into the pocket, hearing echoes of infield jabber as I dreamed of athletic achievement.

During those early years I usually played right field or pitcher, both essentially dispensable positions in a game without strikes and balls, a game in which most batters hit to left field. My tendency to misjudge fly balls was only exceeded by my inability to hit them. Playing well, I later realized, was hereditary. I never knew anyone to improve at it. Those who consistently belted balls over the fence as children continued to do so as adults. Those of us who repeatedly popped out to first base had clearly been born to that station. Yet performance rarely interfered with fantasy. Even after I had matured through the game to spectator I continued to believe that if ever I took up a bat again I would loft balls far out into the bleachers and prance proudly around the bases, my teammates howling their approval.

So that spring morning in my new neighborhood, I finally overcame my reticence and approached a heavyset man sitting on the bench, his T-shirt straining against the overflowing tide of his belly. When I asked him the inning and the score he yelled out to the field, "Anyone know what inning it is?" "Who cares," a short man in knee socks and Bermuda shorts called back from the mound, releasing a slow, arcing pitch toward the plate. "Who's winning?" my contact tried again. "We are," the third baseman said, his eyes fixed upon the batter. "You're dreaming," a fortyish man in knickers and cleats said, swinging two bats in the on-deck circle. "It's five four us, bottom of the fourth." The third baseman shrugged, his eyes still on home plate. "Is it too late to join?" I asked the unthreatening air. "They could use some help," the on-deck batter said, pointing to right field.

Someone threw me a glove, and before I had a chance to reconsider I was jogging out to my old position, nodding hello to the two other men standing in the high grass. One wore a stained white dress shirt with French cuffs that continually needed rolling up, the other a sweatshirt that read, SOFTBALL IS MY ONLY VICE. They nodded their greeting and then turned to face the plate. I did the same, adopting the alert pose of an infielder, ready to secure my reputation and win favor among strangers. On the next pitch the batter popped out to first base and our opponents took the field.

The game, I learned, began at nine every Sunday from the first dry morning in spring to the last weekend in October. Some Sundays the diamond might be crowded with twelve on a side, five men jostling each other in the outfield; other weeks the teams thinned out to only six or seven. Everyone who showed up was welcome to play. The game was relaxed, the competition friendly, the level of skill as varied as the ages of the players. Conditioning, I discovered, had little to do with ability. The heavyset player I had spoken to on the bench routinely drove the ball deep into left field and scrambled around the bases as fleetly as someone half his age and a fraction of his weight.

My own abilities had not seasoned during the years away from the game. The only difference age had made was to increase my susceptibility to pulled muscles. Before the end of that first morning I was limping over an injured right ankle and nursing a sore shoulder, yet reveling in my return to the sport and the easy acceptance I had gained.

I spent that afternoon soaking my battle wounds, proud of every ache and pain. For the first time since moving to the

neighborhood I felt at home. Take a man to any city, put a bat in his hand, and he will feel instantly welcome. He will also feel terribly virtuous, for the mind has a way of amplifying a few seconds of baserunning into a morning of exercise, and of transforming the performance of simple skills into heroics. A single throw in time for the out, one good drive over second base, or a successful leap for a high fly ball can rebuild a shattered ego. In my case, having hit one ball beyond third filled me with satisfaction for the rest of the day.

The next Sunday I returned with my ancient glove, the fingers so stiff and occluded I could barely work my hand into it. By the end of the game it had regained some of its former suppleness, but after twenty years it still seemed too big. I thought of borrowing one, even of buying a new glove, but ultimately rejected the idea. I loved that cracked and dusty mitt and needed something to blame for all my shortcomings as an outfielder.

By the middle of the summer I had become a Sunday morning regular, comfortable enough to rib and be ribbed, taking pleasure in the deliberate chumminess. After a few weeks I knew all the players by name and ceased to think of them as aging, outlandishly dressed executives. Their personalities shone through those outfits. Indeed, when I encountered them on the train, their business suits seemed ill fitting, uncomfortable, even deceitful. Were these the same men who danced and limped, hooted and clapped, shouted and sang in grass-stained ecstasy out there on the diamond?

The following spring Elizabeth was born and suddenly my desire to play softball vanished. Instead I spent Sundays taking her on long walks, introducing her to my favorite haunts. But one morning in September we wandered down to the park just as a game was getting under way.

I thought I would feel a pang of loss finding myself once more on the sidelines. But as a new father I had temporarily lost my need for softball and for the companionship of other men. In time I will probably return to it. Every twenty years seems about right. Perhaps by then I will be able to hit to left field. And maybe too my glove will finally fit.

BEING IN LOVE

First Love

I was barely nine years old when I fell in love for the first time. No one was more surprised than I by my sudden change of feelings. Only a month before I had been punished for bullying the same little girl who now filled me with an unfamiliar tenderness. For weeks I had led a gang of marauding schoolboys in attacks on her and her girlfriends, lifting skirts, pulling hair, stealing books, and hurling insults from the passing school bus. I never denied the charges; I was proud of them and of the anger that overcame me whenever I saw her giggling with her friends. She, with equal venom, taunted me and nimbly dodged my attacks, threatening repeatedly to report me to her parents and to our teacher, a threat she carried out whenever my assaults penetrated her defenses.

But then suddenly the rage turned to love, an almost slavish devotion, and the time I had spent planning my revenges I now devoted to devising means of getting a glimpse of her and concealing such treasons from my friends. I was, it seemed, somewhat premature in my infatuation. Most boys growing up in the fifties did not discover girls until sixth or seventh grade. But there I was in fourth grade, abandoning my faithful comrades in misogyny for an opportunity to sit in a girl's living room and look at her scrapbook while her mother hovered nearby offering ice cream.

Miraculously, that little girl returned my affection, warily at first, then with increasing confidence as I convinced her that my transformation was genuine. During those early months I courted her indoors to avoid being seen by friends and declared a traitor to the cause I had so recently championed. We met in secret at her house, arranged to meet "by accident" at the local five-and-ten on Saturdays, and vigorously denied rumors that we were "going steady," a preposterous condition for fourth graders. Eventually, however, word leaked out and I was made to suffer the ridicule of former allies. But by then I was willing to pay almost any price for love.

In time, however, my friends underwent a similar evolution and began courting girls of their own. I was accepted back into the fold and even occasionally consulted about such delicate issues as hand holding and movie going. Weekends were spent playing touch football with the same girls we had once harassed, while school days raced by in a whirl of secret notes and rumors about new couples. By the end of the year we were all neatly identified in pairs and then the real combat began.

Twelve months later most of the combinations had changed, the dating had become more private, the preening more time-consuming, and broken hearts more common. Phones rang all evening, passions ran high, and in the morning new couples replaced the old. The little girl I had loathed and then loved moved out of my life as I moved out of hers. When we passed each other in the halls of the junior high school and later in senior high, we smiled and nodded in recognition of a shared past, but we had long since discovered far more passionate devotions and had all but lost track of each other's lives.

Ten years elapsed, years of college, career, and marriage, during which so many faces of childhood vanished even from memory. Then we were all called together for a high school reunion, and in the first minutes of that gathering she entered, pregnant with her second child. Was this the same little girl of fourth grade? I wondered, having forgotten what she looked like as a teenager, remembering only the nine-year-old I had fallen in love with so unexpectedly. Suddenly every platitude about time and change overwhelmed me as I approached her and identified myself. With her own exclamation of disbelief she hugged me warmly, then introduced her husband as I presented Nancie. Before the evening ended the four of us made plans to meet again over dinner.

The bond of childhood quickly overcame the awkwardness of so many intervening years. We spent that first meal smiling over shared memories and uttering the same expressions of disbelief about growing older we had heard so often from our parents. Who could have predicted twenty years ago that we would be sitting together with our spouses laughing over the days of hair pulling and touch football? Where had the time gone?

I left that dinner exhilarated by our spontaneous review of the past and by the opportunity to share it with someone who remembered it as I did. We began to meet regularly and soon grew accustomed to each other as adults, concentrating less on memory and more on the present. She talked often of her two boys, as devoted to her family as I remember her mother had been. Nancie and I spoke of our desire, as yet unfulfilled, to begin our own family.

Then one evening, her voice heavy with worry, she called to cancel a dinner engagement. Her younger son had just been hospitalized with a high fever and needed to be monitored continuously. She and her husband were alternating nights at his side and could not say when their life would return to normal.

171

After we hung up I sat for a long while thinking about that call. How was it that the little girl who had first awakened love in me, the little girl whose parents had nursed her through similar childhood illnesses, was now sitting up nights over her own ailing child? In her troubled voice I had just heard the pain of a mother in torment, a pain that seemed to confer parenthood in a way that the simple joys of child rearing did not.

When we next met, her son had fully recovered but her face showed new signs of age, not lines so much as a certain indelible gravity. Her voice had lost some of its lightness, her eyes seemed darker. Although she laughed about the ordeal, I could see that the experience had seared her. She seemed to have discovered how tenuous her happiness was, how crushing life might be, how vulnerable she had become as a parent.

In the spring of the next year Elizabeth was born. Shortly after we brought her home my childhood friend visited with her two boys and looked with special tenderness at the little girl in my arms. "What happened?" she asked, stroking my daughter's cheek. "I thought we were only just children ourselves."

"I was about to ask you the same thing," I replied, standing between her sons. "I certainly don't feel any older."

"What will you do when Elizabeth comes home from school complaining that my boys pulled her hair?" she asked with a gleam of remembrance in her eyes.

"I'll call you to complain, of course," I said, "and I'll expect you to punish them as my parents punished me. And then," I added, "I'll begin counting the days until they fall in love with her."

LOST AT SEA

"The ship's gone down," he muttered with the icy calm of stupefied disbelief. "Vinnie is among the missing—lost at sea."

I had never heard the phrase spoken in connection with someone I knew. The words seemed to resonate with ancient lamentation, Nantucket widows and fatherless children keening for their beloved dead, storm-tossed galleons and raging seas—all wildly misplaced that windless morning in May. How was it possible, in this era of supersonic travel and space exploration, that ships still sank, scattering their crews upon the waves?

I had called Victor on business, unaware that hours earlier the Coast Guard had informed him that his son's ship, a twin-masted schooner, had sunk in a violent thunderstorm, smashed broadside by ninety-mile-an-hour winds. In half a dozen short, bleeding sentences Victor told me that eight of the twelve crew members had been rescued; four, including his son, remained unaccounted for. I listened in stunned silence, embarrassed by my trespass upon his grief, trying futilely to offer comfort. Finally Victor whispered, "I can't talk any longer," and we hung up.

When I called the following morning his wife answered, her voice subdued yet grateful for the opportunity to ease the emptiness of their painful vigil. How long would they be forced to sit by the phone, waiting for the Coast Guard to call, suffering hope each time it rang? How long before the search was abandoned? When I asked if I might visit, she quickly accepted my offer.

An hour later Victor welcomed me, his eyes heavy with sleeplessness. He seemed to have stationed himself somewhere between hope and resignation, prayerful expectation and disappointment, steeling himself for sorrow. As he talked about Vinnie, his tone alternated between mournful remembrance and prideful animation. I was careful to speak of his son only in the present tense, though the feelings and the forms of my visit were couched in condolence.

The sea ran deep within Victor's own blood, he told me. Though he had chosen to cast his lot upon the land, both his father and uncle had captained oceangoing vessels. How could he, then, stand between his son and that destiny? Acutely mindful of the dangers, he nevertheless took pride in Vinnie's courage, in his years as a commercial fisherman off the coast of Maine, and in his fearlessness before the mast, scrambling high into the ship's rigging during even the foulest weather, raising and lowering sails, one of an elite few capable of manning the tall-masted clippers that ran before the wind with quiet grace.

Like countless other parents and wives of seamen down through the ages, Victor had taken his place upon the rack of perpetual worry, scanning the daily papers and the evening news for reports of storms at sea, for any mention of local conflicts that might spill over into the waters bearing his beloved son, his firstborn child. He knew the boy was capable of protecting himself, but like all parents he also understood instinctively that if any harm came to Vinnie he would forever blame himself for not piloting his son into safer waters.

"The nights are the hardest," Victor said as I prepared to leave, his eyes again revealing the pain that had been momentarily eclipsed by fond remembrance. I hesitated on the threshold, hoping to be witness to a miracle, to be present when the blessed call came announcing that Vinnie had been saved, plucked from the sea by the merciful hand of Providence.

But it was not to be. With each passing day the likelihood of locating the missing diminished. From the surviving crew members Victor learned they had been battling rough seas and high winds for several days, setting and trimming the sails in a futile effort to make headway. Finally the storm had seemed to ease, and then suddenly a great "white squall," a freak wind, perhaps a tornado, had blown the craft onto its side. They all recalled shouting, "Come up, come up," but the boat had shipped too much water, sinking in minutes.

All but four succeeded in reaching the single life raft. The captain was last seen struggling to free a second raft tangled in the rigging. Two other crew members were spotted floating helplessly on the waves. Then someone glimpsed Vinnie swimming hard toward his drowning shipmates. The mountainous seas rose and fell, driving the survivors away from the sinking ship, away from the four still hopelessly adrift.

When news of the accident reached shore, Coast Guard cutters and search planes began sweeping a 7,200-square-mile area in the hope of rescuing the missing. What were the chances of survival in those waters? No one would say, not until a week had passed. Then the press begin to whisper, "Missing, presumed dead."

Two weeks later I returned, not to Victor's home but to a

175

nearby chapel, entering the crowded sanctuary as a single cello began to play a doleful, watery dirge. In the front row Victor sat bolt upright, holding his wife's hand, surrounded by friends and relatives, all wishing they could do more to ease the pain than merely share in it. Against the back wall stood several young men in shirtsleeves, ties hastily knotted around sunburned necks. They seemed ill at ease, not because of the church's solemn rites, but because they were newly returned from the sea themselves and had not yet adjusted to the cadences of dry land. They were but a few of the dozens of fishermen with whom Vinnie had sailed, all in their twenties, fearless young men who knew full well the price demanded by the sea for the riches they harvested. Something in their stance bespoke a fatalistic acceptance of death.

Had Victor abandoned all hope, I wondered, listening to the final memorial prayers, or did he still keep alive the image of his son clinging to some fragment of the ship, drifting, endlessly drifting upon the sea? He turned, then, to look out the window, his sharp profile dominated by a single tear-filled eye that seemed to ask, "And what has become of my boy?" His was a death almost as old as man, as vast as the sea, as hollow as the burning emptiness in a bereaved father's breast. It had no place under the fathomless blue sky of a warm May morning in a nation at peace, shattering the green tranquility of a quiet household in the hills of western Connecticut.

BABY BROTHER

He was the last of us, the child of middle age, the fourth and final son, the one whom my father, with his penchant for puns, called "Alice," telling anyone who asked about future children, *"Das is alles."* But he meant far more to me than merely the end of my mother's fertility, more than my parents' futile last attempt to conceive a longed-for daughter. Through him I glimpsed a new world, one as removed from the brutal jealousies of brothers as it was from the youthful, carefree exuberance of my parents' first years of marriage. With his birth I discovered a sort of childlike fatherhood, unfinished yet filled with feelings of unfamiliar tenderness. Having, until that moment, vied with two other brothers for first place in my parents' affections, I suddenly abandoned the struggle, concerned with nothing so much as the well-being of my baby brother.

The eight years that separated us were crucial to the formation of our special bond. At ten, my older brother had begun to turn his attention away from home, preoccupied with friends, sports, and the intoxications of independence, while my three-year-old younger brother felt only indignation at being displaced by a new baby. I, however, had nothing to lose and everything to gain from this addition to our household, desperately needing to shower affection upon someone or something at that moment in my childhood. The instant he entered our home a part of me broke away and took up residence beside him, hovering near the nursery, watching him sleep, feeding him, and occasionally glimpsing that special fear, that vulnerability to loss that only a parent feels.

As a young child he returned my love with medieval fealty, toddling into my room at daybreak, sitting quietly on the floor until I awoke, then climbing onto my bed to wrestle—my self-conscious way of hugging without seeming to hug, an acceptable male substitute for the underlying urge to take him up in my arms and kiss him as if he were my own son. Such open affection between brothers did not come easily in my family. But with this brother I learned, for a time, to overcome my reticence, swept along by his infectious warmth.

Through him I tasted the godlike powers enjoyed by older brothers, swooping down upon his infant battles and carrying him off to safety, then basking in his awe and gratitude. I learned too about self-restraint, taking a poke in the eye or a bite on the leg without anger, absorbing his excesses of energy without deflating his spirit. Above all, I discovered how to communicate without words, conveying through a host of silent sympathies all that he would not yet have understood if expressed in speech.

When I left home for college my little brother moved into my old room, gradually appropriating all I had left behind. Had anyone else presumed to supplant me I would have objected, but I viewed him in some sense as my rightful heir and welcomed his presence among my former possessions, delighted by our common interests. Like a doting father I felt flattered every time he took up one of my favorite hobbies, hoping thereby to preserve our intimacy.

But college made obvious a rift that had begun to form

during my last years in high school. As a teenager, I too drifted away from the family as had my older brother before me. In my absence my little brother found other companionship, other models. Suddenly, the eight years between us served to separate rather than conjoin. He seemed to reach young manhood under a constellation of passions as foreign to me as mine must have seemed to my parents. When I returned home for vacations we groped ineptly for something lost, then abandoned the effort, shaking hands rather than hugging, aware that we had somehow outgrown our childhood attachment.

Despite the distance that had crept in between us, a distance of temperament, taste, and traditions—I was a child of the fifties; he was clearly one of the sixties—I preserved the memory of our mutual devotion, expecting one day to resume it. After he graduated from college we met occasionally in the city to discuss his future. But the easy protection I had offered him as a child did not readily translate into good advice. Mouthing all the clichés of fatherhood without a father's wisdom, I realized I knew nothing of his inner life. So distant did we become that when, two years later, he announced his intention to marry, I was taken completely by surprise.

And then two weeks before his wedding, by a coincidence as sweet as it was unplanned, Elizabeth was born. At a dinner the night before the ceremony, he stood before the assembled relatives and proposed a toast to his niece while she slept in a basket beside the table, the family's first grandchild. That he should be the one to officially welcome her into the family delighted me, he who had first awakened my longing for children twenty-five years earlier. The following day, champagne glass in hand, I stood before his wedding guests and recited the long history of our special closeness, feeling once again both brother and father to him, proud of his transformation to manhood.

Thereafter, through letters and late-night phone calls, we began to communicate regularly, discussing his studies and his niece, gradually repairing the rift. When finally he called to tell me of his wife's pregnancy, I heard the news with something more than an uncle's delight. For just as he had long ago taught me to feel the tenderness of a parent, so I now began to know the special wonder that grandparents speak of when their children produce children of their own.

Six days after my nephew was born I flew south to celebrate his arrival. As I took him from my brother's hands, I recognized something of the dark-haired infant my parents had brought home twenty-five years before. My brother had asked me to conduct the service of welcome that accompanies circumcision, so on my nephew's eighth day I stood between my brother and the doctor, prayer book in hand, feeling him tremble almost imperceptibly at the pain of his son. As I pronounced my nephew's name in Hebrew and English, welcoming him into the covenant of his people, tears came to my brother's eyes. In that moment fatherhood became an overwhelming reality. When, finally, the service ended, he hugged me, loosened his tie, and sat down heavily. He too had discovered the special vulnerability of parents.

A week later he told me over the phone, "I know now what you mean about the breathing." As I had crept into the nursery night after night during Elizabeth's first year, needing constant reassurance that she had not succumbed to some noiseless violence, so he too repeatedly checked on his sleeping son. We talked for an hour, exchanging our perceptions of parenthood, no longer as father and son or even as big and little brother, but as two fathers. And in that exchange I felt a new reality take hold. The years that had first drawn us together and then driven us apart had once again been bridged. Through the medium of our children we had recaptured the instinctive harmony of the past, rediscovering a sympathy beyond words.

TWINS AT TWO

Most mornings now the twins come bursting out of the nursery shouting an exuberant good morning, their fat little legs just barely keeping pace with their explosive enthusiasm. They want to jump on our bed, hide in the closet, stumble about in my loafers, comb their hair with our toothbrushes. They want to be tickled, kissed, tossed in the air, to be anything but hugged, not if it means holding still, even for a moment. They have no patience for stasis; there is entirely too much to do, too much to see. Around them stands an entire house waiting to be pulled apart. They are determined to get a jump on the chaos: so much havoc to wreak, so little time.

"Breakfast," Juliana declares, taking my hand and leading me to the stairs. She is more thoughtful than her twin brother, more cautious, more verbal. Seeing us depart, David runs ahead, drops to his belly, and slides hell-bent down the stairs, disappearing beneath the dining room table, mischief writ large across his grinning face. Within the last few weeks, it seems, they both abandoned babyhood,

181

striding square-shouldered and secure into the thicket of complex language, discrete personality, and humor. Overnight they became what, in Yiddish, one would call *"menschen,"* thoughtful, well-intentioned little people: budding, benevolent, full of laughter, capable of scheming to achieve what they want, of manipulating, of even occasionally taking no for an answer, but most of all filled with love and a boundless desire to express it. Twins at two, Nancie and I have decided, are nothing short of delicious.

Of course, it wasn't always this delightful. The first six, sleepless months were shattering, unnerving. Night after relentless night I lay down in terror, knowing the next cry would come just as sleep took hold, jarring me back into a stumbling, nauseous wakefulness, initiating yet another exhausting round of bottles, diapers, and interminable rocking. Friends later told me I seemed to have aged ten years in as many harrowing weeks. Sleep deprivation is the quickest route I know to blithering idiocy. I was fast becoming a vacant vessel, feeling as if someone had tapped a vein and left it open, the substance of my being slowly transfused into the babies, giving them life, leaving me bloodless, empty, enervated. I felt like a salmon consuming itself in the desperate, terminal effort to swim upstream and spawn. So this is what they meant when they warned that nothing aged one quite like the raising of children. The expenditure of energy required for basic care in duplicate, for diapering, dressing, and feeding two (not to mention their two-year-old sister), was greater than we were able to recoup during the three or four hours of intermittent sleep the twins allowed us each night. And so, gradually, we wound down, falling prey to every virus, every sniffle, every cough, wondering what had become of our youth, of the pleasure we once took from life, from children, from each other.

And then, just as we thought we might lose our minds, staring bleary-eyed and motionless before ringing telephones and persistent doorbells, trying to remember what was expected of us, life began to improve. At four months Juliana slept through the night, at six months David. The weather turned warm, we shucked off the last of our winter colds, threw open the doors, and introduced the twins to the great green beyond. Sturdy enough now to withstand the glancing blows of their well-intentioned but often too aggressive older sister, they could be left to graze in the garden beyond the kitchen windows while we lingered over breakfast probing our cerebral extremities, seeking signs of intelligent life. For six months we hadn't watched a movie, read a book, engaged in anything resembling meaningful conversation. But now, miraculously, thought returned. Yes, Virginia, there is life after twins (albeit remedial, tentative, intermittent), and where there's life, there's hope.

In short order the raising of David and Juliana passed from exhausting ordeal to exhilarating orgy, from arduous labor to ardent delight. We watched in fascination as they began to differentiate themselves, fashioning their own unique responses to the world. David's proved, in stunning confirmation of sexual stereotyping, to be largely physical; Juliana's primarily verbal. While they acquired many skills within hours of each other: rolling over, mumbling their first, barely intelligible word, taking an inaugural spoonful of gruel; other milestones were reached weeks, even months apart. David broke the bonds of gravity long before his sister, walking with slap-footed bravado across the living room, arms raised, eyes twinkling, while Juliana crawled after him, still tethered hand and foot. She, on the other hand, began spilling torrents of melodic gibberish from her tiny, toothless mouth, while he remained largely mute, content to babble an occasional "Mommy" or simply to grunt.

So rapidly did matters improve that by their first birthday I found myself seriously contemplating having yet another child. I had always wanted four or five, never stopping to consider the emotional, physical, or financial cost of such procreative depravity. And now once again, barely recovered from the trauma of twins, I began telling myself, "It wasn't so terrible, was it?" Apparently, postpartum amnesia is not confined to mothers.

But Nancie's memory was not nearly so selective. "Any subsequent children," she calmly replied, spoon-feeding mashed bananas into two reluctant faces, "will have to come from your next wife." Her tone suggested that this sudden desire of mine was more a measure of madness—probably a delayed side effect of all those sleepless nights—than of anything corresponding to reality, especially knowing, as I did, that the odds of conceiving twins increases fourfold after a multiple pregnancy. But even the prospect of leapfrogging from three to five children did not deter me. When I considered packing up the cribs and giving away all those diminutive outfits, not to mention the rattles, the readers, and the rocking chairs, I found myself wishing for just one more go-round, one last chance to stand giddy and groggy-eyed over a sleeping infant. A single child would be a piece of cake, I told Nancie, hardly noticeable in the general mayhem, just one more happy face to feed. And even twins wouldn't be so tough this time around. We were veterans, after all; we'd finally gotten it down to a science.

"In case you've forgotten," Nancie reminded me, "my ninth month was interminable agony." Yes, I had forgotten: the hours spent in the tub in search of buoyancy, the six weeks in bed, the swollen ankles, the perpetual heartburn, the inflamed gallbladder, and the fourteen pounds of living, kicking babyhood pressing on her every vital organ. Under similar conditions I probably would have slit my wrists. No, I realized with regret, it would not be sporting to expose her again to such torture. I would have to content myself with three.

But then shortly before the twins' second birthday, I found her jotting down names on a scrap of paper, children's names, some of the very ones we had considered the first two times around. Seeing me peer over her shoulder, she smiled sheepishly and shrugged. So the door wasn't shut after all. My suggestion, it seemed, had found a narrow corner of fertile ground amid all the concrete of her resistance. Perhaps with proper tending, I might just coax new life from that tiny quadrant. She seemed to be challenging me to try.

Her reversal shouldn't have come as a surprise; we're both gluttons for punishment. More important, the twins at two have become the most persuasive reason I know for having another child. Like most second children, they are more malleable than their headstrong older sister, more even tempered, more responsive. To a great extent they are raising themselves, watching each other, their big sister, and us for clues. They don't require the constant attention we assumed Elizabeth needed; they have each other. Though we are occasionally called upon to provide reassurance, to smooth a bent psyche when floor unexpectedly meets forehead, most of the learning goes on without us. With our first child we felt a mixture of impotence and invincibility, terrified by life's capriciousness, yet convinced that if given grace enough and time we could effect miracles. With the coming of the twins we have let go of both poles, less fearful of fate, no longer preoccupied with creating perfect children. They seem content to explore their universe like two rogue meteors, crashing through our atmosphere momentarily for a kiss or a brief hello, then continuing on their wayward journey into outer space, leaving an incandescent tail of debris behind them.

And so it was this morning as David disappeared beneath the dining room table, giggling at his cleverness.

"Where's your brother?" I ask Juliana.

"Davey hiding," she responds with hungry nonchalance, pulling me past him to the kitchen. "Want cottage cheese, want Cheerios, want steak," she demands as I lift her into the high chair.

The last of the three gives me pause. Steak? We rarely serve red meat in our house, and certainly never for breakfast. Where did she get such an idea? I decide to ignore the request and offer a double portion of Cheerios. But no sooner do I join her at the table than she repeats her request, intoned this time more as a demand: "Want steak, Daddy."

"We have no steak," I reply, wondering if I am hearing correctly. It wasn't so long ago that I couldn't understand three quarters of what she said. Juliana points toward the pantry closet and bellows "Steak," her patience growing thin, her eyes beginning to redden. Any idiot, she seems to be saying, should be able to understand this request.

"I don't know what you mean," I respond, opening the pantry, the willing slave of this three-foot tyrant. The shelves are crowded with cereals, canned soups, spaghetti, jam, soda. Juliana points to an upper shelf and repeats her demand. When I lift the Pop Tarts she shakes her head. I point to the marshmallows, she scowls; the chocolate chip cookies, she glowers; the macaroni and cheese, she screams, "No! Steak!"

Then, finally, my eyes light on the potato chips, or in this case, the steak fries, as the particular brand is called. Aha! How quickly the sins of the fathers are visited upon the children. She has not forgotten her dinner treat, the few chips she was rewarded after finishing her mixed vegetables.

"Later," I tell her, trying to maintain some order amid the general chaos of her diet, "for lunch."

But expecting deferred gratification from a two-year-old makes about as much sense as lobbying her mother for a second set of twins. It's steak or nothing, she declares, holding her bottle high above her head, a miniature Moses poised to hurl the tablets of the law. When I close the pantry without removing the chips, she does exactly that,

shouting, "Want steak!" sweeping her arms across her high-chair tray, flinging Cheerios onto the floor. Welcome to the terrible twos.

I leave her simmering awhile and attempt to retrieve her brother from beneath the table. He evades my arms, laughing, taunting me with Cheshire-like smiles, peeping out between the legs of chairs, then rapidly retreating. He is an extraordinarily affectionate child, carefree, explorative, impulsive, capable of following a straight line into the unknown without so much as a glance back, convinced that the universe is nothing more than a benevolent bauble created for his amusement.

And then four-year-old Elizabeth joins the fray, rushing to the kitchen to see what's the matter with her bellowing younger sister. When I hear the sound of the step stool being dragged across the floor, followed by the crinkling of plastic, I can guess what is going on. Juliana's crying stops. And then, while I struggle in vain to extricate David, Elizabeth enters the dining room carrying the potato chip bag, which she waves beneath the table, easily enticing her little brother into the kitchen.

And then all three of them are seated at the table, milk and cereal and potato chips before them, sharing a joke, trying, at Elizabeth's suggestion, to balance the steak fries on their noses, laughing hysterically each time the chips fall. And once again I find myself thinking: delicious children, I wouldn't mind a few more.